Creative Criticism

AND OTHER ESSAYS

Creative Criticism

AND OTHER ESSAYS

BY J. E. SPINGARN

A NEW AND ENLARGED EDITION

KENNIKAT PRESS, INC./PORT WASHINGTON, N. Y.

CREATIVE CRITICISM
Copyright 1917 by Henry Holt and Company
Copyright 1925, 1931 by J.E. Spingarn
This edition published by Kennikat Press by arrangement
with Harcourt, Brace and World, Inc. 1964

Library of Congress Catalog Card No: 64-24469

Manufactured in the United States of America

Prefatory Note

THE essays collected in 1917 under the title of *Creative Criticism: Essays on the Unity of Genius and Taste* are now out of print, and I have been asked to prepare a new edition of them. I do so with some reluctance, for the essays were written between 1910 and 1913, and naturally do not adequately represent my present opinions. But since they have been preserved so long by their detractors, and may perhaps have some slight interest as representing one of the stages or aspects of American criticism, I have decided to let them live a little longer; and I have added four other essays on kindred subjects, written immediately after the War, between 1921 and 1923. In most of these, too, though I march in a somewhat different direction, I have the temerity to wear, I hope for the last time, the same flowing vaticinal robes. I have also added some illustrative documents in an Appendix.

The whole of *Creative Criticism* has been re-

Prefatory Note

printed in Part I, with the exception of "A Note on Genius and Taste" which has seemed to me too slight to reprint. The first paper, "The New Criticism," was delivered as a public lecture at Columbia University in March, 1910, and was first published in the *Columbia University Lectures on Literature* in 1911; it has undergone slight revision as it has been successively reprinted, and assumed a more or less final form in *Criticism in America: Its Function and Status.* "Prose and Verse" was first published in *Creative Criticism,* and "Dramatic Criticism and the Theatre" in the fourth volume of *Essays and Studies by Members of the English Association* (Oxford, Clarendon Press, 1913). "Creative Connoisseurship" was originally written as a letter to an artist friend, and was printed in the New York *Evening Post* in February, 1913.

Of the four papers in Part II, the first, "The Younger Generation: A New Manifesto," appeared in the *Freeman* in June, 1922, and was reprinted in a slightly revised form in *Troutbeck Leaflets* in 1925; the "fashionable theory" which

Prefatory Note

it attacks has gone the way of all fashionable theories, but the main argument is unaffected by this fact. "The American Critic" was originally part of an article on "Scholarship and Criticism" in *Civilization in the United States: An Inquiry by Thirty Americans* in 1922, and was somewhat modified when it was reprinted as a separate essay in *Criticism in America: Its Function and Status* in 1924. "The American Scholar: A Lament," a lyrical *cri du cœur* rather than a critical statement of the case, formed part of the same article in *Civilization in the United States*. "The Growth of a Literary Myth" appeared in the *Freeman* in May, 1923.

The papers in the Appendix are of a different character, and are reprinted as a matter of record. "Non Credo" appeared as a letter to the editor in the *New Republic* in January, 1925. The "Notes on the New Humanism" were published in the *Journal of Philosophy, Psychology, and Scientific Methods* in December, 1913, and June, 1914, and the "Note on French Scholarship" in the *Romanic Review* of January, 1926. "The Seven Arts and the Seven Confusions," which was written at about the same time as "The New Criticism," is reprinted from the *Seven Arts* of March, 1917.

J. E. S.

TROUTBECK, *April, 1931.*

Contents

PART I. CREATIVE CRITICISM

THE NEW CRITICISM   3

PROSE AND VERSE   39

DRAMATIC CRITICISM AND THE THEATRE   52

CREATIVE CONNOISSEURSHIP   94

PART II. OTHER ESSAYS

THE YOUNGER GENERATION: A NEW MANI-
    FESTO   109

THE AMERICAN CRITIC   123

THE AMERICAN SCHOLAR   148

THE GROWTH OF A LITERARY MYTH   162

APPENDIX

NON CREDO   181

NOTES ON THE NEW HUMANISM (1913-14)   184

A NOTE ON FRENCH SCHOLARSHIP   200

THE SEVEN ARTS AND THE SEVEN CON-
    FUSIONS   210

Part I

CREATIVE CRITICISM

ESSAYS ON THE UNITY OF GENIUS AND TASTE

"Criticism is a practice of the Moderns. What does this mean? Just this: If you read a book and let it work upon you, and yield yourself up entirely to its influence, then, and only then, will you arrive at a correct judgment of it."—GOETHE.

The New Criticism

"WHAT droll creatures these college professors are whenever they talk about art," wrote Flaubert in one of his letters, and voiced the world's opinion of academic criticism. For the world shares the view of the Italian poet that "monks and professors cannot write the lives of poets," and looks only to those rich in literary experience for its opinions on literature. But the poets themselves have had no special grudge against academic criticism that they have not felt equally for every other kind. For the most part, they have objected to all criticism, since what each mainly seeks in his own case is not criticism, but uncritical praise. "Kill the dog, he is a reviewer," cried the young Goethe; and in an age nearer our own William Morris expressed his contempt for those who earn a livelihood by writing their opinions of the works of others. Fortunately for Criticism, it does not live by the grace of poets, to whom it can be of small service at its best, but

3

by the grace of others who have neither the poet's genius nor the critic's insight. I hope to persuade you this evening that the poets have been mistaken in their very conception of the critic's craft, which lives by a power that poets and critics share together. The secret of this power has come to men slowly, and the knowledge they have gained by it has transformed their idea of Criticism. What this secret is, and into what new paths Criticism is being led by it, is the subject of my lecture tonight.

I

AT THE end of the last century, France once more occupied the centre of that stage whose auditors are the inheritors of European civilisation. Once more all the world listened while she talked and played, and some of the most brilliant of her talk was now on the question of the authority of Criticism. It is not my purpose to tell you (what you know already) with what sober and vigorous learning the official critics of the *Revue des deux Mondes* espoused the cause of old gods with the new weapons of science, and with what charm and tact, with what grace and suppleness of thought, Jules Lemaître and Anatole France, to mention no others, defended the free play of the appreciative mind. Some of the sparks that were beaten out on the anvil of controversy have become fixed stars, the classical utterances of Criticism, as when Anatole France described the critic not as a judge imposing sentence, but as a sensitive soul detailing his "adventures among masterpieces."

To have sensations in the presence of a work of art and to express them, that is the function of Criticism for the impressionistic critic. His attitude he would express somewhat in this fashion: "Here is a beautiful poem, let us say Shelley's *Prometheus Unbound*. To read it is for me to experience a thrill of pleasure. My delight in it is itself a judgment, and what better judgment is it possible for me to give? All that I can do is to tell how it affects me, what sensations it gives me. Other men will derive other sensations from it, and express them differently; they too have the same right as I. Each of us, if we are sensitive to impressions and express ourselves well, will produce a new work of art to replace the work which gave us our sensations. That is the art of Criticism, and beyond that Criticism cannot go."

We shall not begrudge this exquisite soul the pleasure of his sensations or his cult of them, nor would he be disconcerted if we were to point out that the interest has been shifted from the work of art to his own impressions. Let us suppose that you say to him: "We are not interested in you, but in *Prometheus Unbound*. To describe the state of your health is not to help us to understand or to enjoy the poem. Your criticism constantly tends to get away from the work of art, and to centre attention on yourself and your feelings."

But his answer would not be difficult to find: "What you say is true enough. My criticism tends to get farther and farther from the work of art and to cast a light upon myself; but all criticism tends to get away from the work of art and to substitute something in its place. The impressionist substitutes himself, but what other form of criticism gets closer to *Prometheus Unbound*? Historical criticism takes us away from it in a search of the environment, the age, the race, the poetic

6

school of the artist; it tells us to read the history of the French Revolution, Godwin's *Political Justice*, the *Prometheus Bound* of Aeschylus, and Calderón's *Mágico Prodigioso*. Psychological criticism takes me away from the poem, and sets me to work on the biography of the poet; I wish to enjoy *Prometheus Unbound*, and instead I am asked to become acquainted with Shelley the man. Dogmatic criticism does not get any closer to the work of art by testing it according to rules and standards; it sends me to the Greek dramatists, to Shakespeare, to Aristotle's *Poetics*, possibly to Darwin's *Origin of Species*, in order that I may see how far Shelley has failed to give dramatic reality to his poem, or has failed to observe the rules of his *genre;* but that means the study of other works, and not of *Prometheus Unbound*. Aesthetics takes me still farther afield into speculations on art and beauty. And so it is with every form of Criticism. Do not deceive yourself. All criticism tends to shift the interest from the work of art to something else. The other critics give us history, politics, biography, erudition, metaphysics. As for me, I re-dream the poet's dream, and if I seem to write lightly, it is because I have awakened, and smile to think I have mistaken a dream for reality. I at least strive to replace one work of art by another, and art can only find its *alter ego* in art."

It would be idle to detail the arguments with which the advocates of the opposing forms of Criticism answered these questionings. Literary erudition and evolutionary science were the chief weapons used to fight this modern heresy, but the one is an unwieldy and the other a useless weapon in the field of aesthetic thought. On some sides, at least, the position of the impressionists was impregnable; but two points of attack were open to their opponents. They could combat the notion that taste is a substitute for learning, or learning a substitute for taste, since both are vital for Criticism; and they could maintain that the relativity of taste does not in any sense affect its authority. In this sense impressionistic Criticism erred only less grievously than the "judicial" Criticism which opposed it. Each in its own way was inadequate and incomplete.

But these arguments are not my present concern; what I wish to point out is that the objec-

tive and dogmatic forms of Criticism were fight-
ing no new battle against impressionistic Criticism
in that decade of controversy. It was a battle as
old as the earliest reflection on the subject of
poetry, if not as old as the sensitiveness of poets.
Modern literature begins with the same doubts,
with the same quarrel. In the sixteenth century the
Italians were formulating that classical code which
imposed itself on Europe for two centuries, and
which, even in our generation, Brunetière has
merely disguised under the trappings of natural
science. They evolved the dramatic unities, and all
those rules which the poet Pope imagined to be
"Nature still but Nature methodised." But at the
very moment when their spokesman Scaliger was
saying that "Aristotle is our emperor, the perpetual dictator of all the fine arts," another Italian, Pietro Aretino, was insisting that there is no
rule except the whim of genius and no standard of
judgment beyond individual taste.

The Italians passed on the torch to the French
of the seventeenth century, and from that day to
this the struggle between the two schools has never
ceased to agitate the progress of Criticism in

France. Boileau against Saint-Evremond, Classicists against Romanticists, dogmatists against impressionists,—the antinomy is deep in the French nature, indeed in the nature of Criticism itself. Listen to this: "It is not for the purpose of deciding on the merit of this noble poet [Virgil], nor of harming his reputation, that I have spoken so freely concerning him. The world will continue to think what it does of his beautiful verses; and as for me, I judge nothing, I only say what I think, and what effect each of these things produces on my heart and mind." Surely these words are from the lips of Lemaître himself! "I judge nothing; I only say what I feel." But no, these are the utterances of the Chevalier de Méré, a wit of the age of Louis XIV, and he is writing to the secretary of that stronghold of authority, the French Academy. For some men, even in the age of Boileau, criticism was nothing but an "adventure among masterpieces."

No, it is no new battle; it is the perpetual conflict of Criticism. In every age impressionism (or enjoyment) and dogmatism (or judgment) have grappled with one another. They are the two sexes of Criticism; and to say that they flourish in every age is to say that every age has its masculine as well as its feminine criticism,—the masculine criticism that may or may not force its own standards on literature, but that never at all events is dominated by the object of its studies; and the feminine criticism that responds to the lure of art with a kind of passive ecstasy. In the age of Boileau it was the masculine type which gave the tone to Criticism; in our own, outside of the universities, it has certainly been the feminine. But they continue to exist side by side, ever falling short of their highest powers, unless mystically mated,—judgment erecting its edicts into arbitrary standards and conventions, enjoyment lost in the mazes of its sensuous indecision.

Yet if we examine these opposing forms of Criticism in our own age, we shall find, I think, that they are not wholly without a common ground to meet on; that, in fact, they are united in at least one prepossession which they do not share with the varying forms of Criticism in any of the earlier periods of its history. The Greeks conceived of literature, not as an inevitable expression of creative power, but as a reasoned "imitation" or re-shaping of the materials of life; for Aristotle, poetry is the result of man's imitative instinct, and differs from history and science in that it deals with the probable or possible rather than with the real. The Romans conceived of literature as a noble art, intended (though under the guise of pleasure) to inspire men with high ideals of life. The classicists of the sixteenth and seventeenth centuries accepted this view in the main; for them, literature was a kind of exercise,—a craft acquired by study of the classics, and guided in the interpretation of nature by the traditions of Greek and Roman art. For these men literature was as much a product of reason as science or history. The eighteenth century complicated the course of Criticism by the introduction of vague and novel criteria, such as "imagination," "sentiment," and "taste," yet it was only in part able to liberate itself from the older tradition.

But with the Romantic Movement there developed the new idea which co-ordinates all Criticism in the nineteenth century. Very early in the century, Mme. de Staël and others formulated the

idea that literature is an "expression of society"—
a phrase that is merely a half-truth if "society"
is interpreted in terms of the narrow circle of the
individual poet's life instead of in terms of that
society which is commensurate with the spirit of
man. Victor Cousin enunciated "the fundamental
rule, that expression is the supreme law of art,"
and, as the meaning of expression was gradually
misunderstood and narrowed, became the unwit-
ting parent of the mechanical theories of the
French school of "art for art's sake." Later, Sainte-
Beuve developed and illustrated his theory that
literature is an expression of personality—another
misleading half-truth, if by personality is meant,
not the artistic personality which unfolds itself in
the work of art, but the complex of external traits
which the artist exhibits in his practical life. Still
later, under the influence of natural science, Taine
took a hint from Hegel and elaborated the idea
that literature is an expression of race, age, and
environment. The extreme impressionists prefer
to think of art as the exquisite expression of delicate and fluctuating sensations or impressions of
life. But for all these critics and theorists, litera-

ture is an expression of something, of experience or emotion, of the external or internal, of the man himself or something outside the man; yet it is always conceived of as an art of expression. The objective, the dogmatic, the impressionistic critics of our day may set for themselves very different tasks, but the idea of expression is implicit in all they write.

French criticism has been leaning heavily on the idea of expression for a century or more, but no attempt has been made in France to understand its aesthetic content, except for a few vague echoes of German thought. For the first to give philosophic precision to the theory of expression, and to found a method of Criticism based upon it, were the Germans of the age that stretches from Herder to Hegel. All the forces of philosophical thought were focussed on this central concept, while the critics enriched themselves from out this golden store. I suppose you all remember the famous passage in which Carlyle describes the achievement of German criticism in that age. "Criticism," says Carlyle, "has assumed a new form in Germany. It proceeds on other principles and proposes to itself a higher aim. The main question is not now a question concerning the qualities of diction, the coherence of metaphors, the fitness of sentiments, the general logical truth in a work of art, as it was some half century ago among most critics, neither is it a question mainly of a psychological sort to be answered by discovering and delineating the peculiar nature of the poet from his poetry, as is usual with the best of our own critics at present; but it is, not indeed exclusively, but inclusively, of its two other questions, properly and ultimately a question of the essence and peculiar life of the poetry itself. . . . The problem is not now to determine by what mechanism Addison composed sentences and struck out similitudes, but by what far finer and more mysterious mechanism Shakespeare organised his dramas and gave life and individuality to his Ariel and his Hamlet. Wherein lies that life; how have they attained that shape and individuality? Whence comes that empyrean fire which irradiates their whole being, and pierces, at least in starry gleams, like a diviner thing, into all hearts? Are these dramas of his not verisimilar only, but true; nay, truer than reality itself, since the essence of unmixed reality is bodied forth in them under more expressive similes? What is this unity of pleasures; and can our deeper inspection discern it to be indivisible and existing by necessity because each work springs as it were from the general elements of thought and grows up therefrom into form and expansion by its own growth? Not only who was the poet and how did he compose, but what and how was the poem, and why was it a poem and not rhymed eloquence, creation and not figured passion? These are the questions for the critic. Criticism stands like an interpreter between the inspired and the uninspired; between the prophet and those who hear the melody of his words, and catch some glimpse of their material meaning, but understand not their deeper import."

I am afraid that no German critic wholly realised this ideal; but it was at least the achievement of the Germans that they enunciated the doctrine, even if they did not always adequately illustrate it in practice. It was they who first realised that art has performed its function when it has expressed itself; it was they who first conceived of Criticism as the study of expression. "There is a destructive and a creative or constructive criticism," said Goethe; the first measures and tests literature according to mechanical standards, the second answers the fundamental questions: "What has the writer proposed to himself to do? and how far has he succeeded in carrying out his own plan?" Carlyle, in his essay on Goethe, almost uses Goethe's own words, when he says that the critic's first and foremost duty is to make plain to himself "what the poet's aim really and truly was, how the task he had to do stood before his eye, and how far, with such materials as were afforded him, he has fulfilled it."

This has been the central problem, the guiding star, of all modern criticism. From Coleridge to Pater, from Sainte-Beuve to Lemaître, this is what critics have been striving for, even when they have not succeeded; yes, even when they have been deceiving themselves into thinking that they were striving for something else. This was not the ideal of the critics of Aristotle's day, who, like so many of their successors, censured a work of art as "irrational, impossible, morally hurtful, self-contradictory, or contrary to technical correctness." This was

not Boileau's standard when he blamed Tasso for
the introduction of Christian rather than pagan
mythology into epic poetry; nor Addison's, when
he tested *Paradise Lost* according to the rules of
Le Bossu; nor Dr. Johnson's, when he lamented
the absence of poetic justice in *King Lear*, or pro-
nounced dogmatically that the poet should not
"number the streaks of the tulip." What has the
poet tried to do, and how has he fulfilled his intention? What is he striving to express and how
has he expressed it? What vital and essential spirit
animates his work, what central impression does
it leave on the receptive mind, and how can I best
express this impression? Is his work true to the
laws of its own being rather than to laws formulated by others? These are the questions that modern critics have been taught to ask when face to
face with the work of a poet. Only one *caveat*
must be borne in mind when attempting to answer
them: the poet's aim must be judged at the moment of the creative act, that is to say, by the art
of the poem itself, and not by the vague ambitions which he imagines to be his real intentions
before or after the creative act is achieved. For to

create a work of art is the goal of every artist; and all questions in regard to his achievement are merely different ways of asking, different ways of helping to answer, the one supreme question: Has he or has he not created a work of art?

II

THE theory of expression, the concept of literature as an art of expression, is the common ground on which critics have met for a century or more. Yet how many absurdities, how many complicated systems, how many confusions have been superimposed on this fundamental idea; and how slowly has its full significance become the possession of critics! To accept the naked principle is to play havoc with these confusions and complications; and no one has seen this more clearly, or driven home its inevitable consequences with more intelligence and vigour, than an Italian thinker and critic of our own day, Benedetto Croce, who has been gaining ground in the English-speaking world from the day when Mr. Balfour several years ago gave him a kind of official introduction in his Romanes Lecture. But I for one needed no introduction to his work; under his banner I enrolled myself long ago, and here re-enroll myself in what I now say. He has led aesthetic thought inevitably from the concept that art is expression to the conclusion that all expression is art. Time does not permit, nor reason ask, that we should follow this argument through all its *pros* and *cons*. If this theory of expression be once and for all accepted, as indeed it has been partly though confusedly accepted by all modern critics, the ground of Criticism is cleared of its dead lumber and its weeds. I propose now merely to point out this dead lumber and these weeds. In other words, we shall see to what conclusions the critical thought and practice of a century have been inevitably converging, and what elements of the old Criticism and the old literary history are disappearing from the new.

In the first place, we have done with all the old Rules. The very conception of "rules" harks back to an age of magic, and reminds the modern of those mysterious words which the heroes of the fairy-tales are without reason forbidden to utter;

the rules are a survival of the savage *taboo*. We find few arbitrary rules in Aristotle, who limited himself to empirical inductions from the experience of literature; but they appear in the later Greek rhetoricians; and in the Romans, empirical induction has been hardened into dogma. Horace lays down the law to the prospective playwright in this manner: "You must never have more than three actors on the stage at any one time; you must never let your drama have more or less than five acts." It is unnecessary to trace the history of these rules, or to indicate how they increased in number, how they were arranged into a system by the classicists of the sixteenth and seventeenth centuries, and how they burdened the creative art of that period. They were never without their enemies. We have seen how Aretino was pitted against Scaliger, Saint-Evremond against Boileau; and in every age the poets have astounded the critics by transgressing rules without the sacrifice of beauty; but it was not until the end of the eighteenth century that the Romanticists banished them from the province of Criticism. The pedantry of our own day has borrowed "conventions" from history and "technique" from science as substitutes for the outworn formulae of the past; but these are merely new names for the old mechanical rules; and they too will go, when Criticism clearly recognises in every work of art a spiritual creation governed by its own law.

We have done with the *genres*, or literary kinds. Their history is inseparably bound up with that of the classical rules. Certain works of literature have a general resemblance and are loosely classed together (for the sake of convenience) as lyric, comedy, tragedy, epic, pastoral, and the like; the classicists made of each of these divisions a fixed norm governed by inviolable laws. The separation of the *genres* was a consequence of this law of classicism: comedy should not be mingled with tragedy, nor epic with lyric. But no sooner was the law enunciated than it was broken by an artist impatient or ignorant of its restraints, and the critics have been obliged to explain away these violations of their laws, or gradually to change the laws themselves. But if art is organic expression, and every work of art is to be interrogated with the question, "What has it expressed, and how completely?" there is no place for the question whether it has conformed to some convenient classification of critics or to some law derived from this classification. The lyric, the pastoral, the epic, are abstractions without concrete reality in the world of art. Poets do not really write epics, pastorals, lyrics, however much they may be deceived by these false abstractions; they express themselves, and this expression is their only form. There are not, therefore, only three, or ten, or a hundred literary kinds; there are as many kinds as there are individual poets. But it is in the field of literary history that this error is most obvious. Shakespeare wrote *King Lear, Venus and Adonis,* and a sequence of sonnets. What becomes of Shakespeare, the creative artist, when these three works are separated from one another by the historian of poetry; when they lose their connection with his single creative soul, and are classified with other works with which they have only a loose and vague relation? To slice up the history of English literature into compartments marked comedy, tragedy, lyric, and the like, is to be guilty of a complete misunderstanding of the meaning of Criticism; and literary history becomes a logical absurdity when its data are not organically related but cut up into sections, and placed in such compartments as these. Only in one sense has any of these terms any profound significance, and that is the use of the word "lyric" to represent the free expressiveness of art. All art is lyrical—the *Divine Comedy*, *King Lear*, Rodin's "Thinker," the Parthenon, a Corot landscape, a Bach fugue, or Isadora Duncan's dancing, as much as the songs of Heine or Shelley.

We have done with the comic, the tragic, the sublime, and an army of vague abstractions of their kind. These have grown out of the generalisations of the Alexandrian critics, acquiring a new lease of life in the eighteenth century. Gray and his friend West corresponded with each other on the subject of the sublime; later, Schiller distinguished between the naïve and the sentimental; Jean Paul defined humour, and Hegel defined the tragic. If these terms represent the content of art, they may be relegated to the same category as joy, hate, sorrow, enthusiasm; and we should speak of the comic in the same general way in which we might speak of the expression of joy in a poem. If, on the other hand, these terms represent abstract classifications of poetry, their use in criticism sins against the very nature of art. Every poet re-expresses the universe in his own way, and every poem is a new and independent expression. The tragic does not exist for Criticism, but only Aeschylus and Calderón, Shakespeare and Racine. There is no objection to the use of the word tragic as a convenient label for somewhat similar poems, but to find laws for the tragic and to test creative artists by such laws as these is simply to give a more abstract form to the outworn classical conception of dramatic rules.

We have done with the theory of style, with metaphor, simile, and all the paraphernalia of Graeco-Roman rhetoric. These owe their existence to the assumption that style is separate from expression, that it is something which may be added or subtracted at will from the work of art, a flourish of the pen, an external embellishment, instead of the poet's individual vision of reality, the music of his whole manner of being. But we know that art *is* expression, that it is complete in itself, that to alter it is to create another expression and therefore to create another work of art. If the poet, for example, says of springtime that " 'Tis now the blood runs gold," he has not employed a substitute for something else, such as "the blood tingles in our veins"; he has expressed his thought in its completeness, and there is no equivalent for his expression except itself.

> "Each perfect in its place; and each content
> With that perfection which its being meant."

Such expressions are still called metaphors in the text-books; but metaphor, simile, and all the old terms of classical rhetoric are signs of the zodiac, magical incantations, astrological formulae, interesting only to antiquarian curiosity. To Montaigne they suggested "the prattle of chambermaids"; to me they suggest rather the drone and singsong of many schoolmistresses. We still hear talk of the "grand style," and essays on style continue to be written, like the old "arts of poetry" of two centuries ago. But the theory of styles has no longer a real place in modern thought; we have learned that it is no less impossible to study style as separate from the work of art than to study the comic as separate from the work of the comic artist.

We have done with all moral judgment of art as art. Horace said that pleasure and profit are the function or end of poetry, and for many centuries the critics quarrelled over the terms "pleasure" and "profit." Some said that poetry was meant to instruct; some, merely to please; some, to do both. Romantic criticism first enunciated the principle that art has no aim except expression; that its aim is complete when expression is complete; that "beauty is its own excuse for being." It is not the inherent function of poetry to further any moral or social cause, any more than it is the function of bridge-building to further the cause of Esperanto. The historian, the philosopher, the legislator, may legitimately consider a work of art, not as a work of art, but as a social document, just as the quarryman may consider a statue merely as so many pounds of marble, but in so doing they must realize that they are ignoring its essential purpose and the fundamental source of its power. For if the achievement of the poet be to express any material he may select, and to express it with a completeness that we recognise as perfection, obviously morals can play no part in the judgment which Criticism may form of this artistic achievement. To say that poetry, as poetry, is moral or immoral is as meaningless as to say that an equilateral triangle is moral and an isosceles triangle immoral, or to speak of the immorality of a musical chord or a Gothic arch. It is only conceivable in a world in which dinner-table conversation runs after this fashion: "This cauliflower would be good if it had only been prepared in accordance with international law." "Do you know why my cook's pastry is so good? Because he has never told a lie or seduced a woman." We do not concern ourselves with morals when we test the engineer's bridge or the scientist's researches; indeed we go farther, and say that it is the moral duty of the scientist to disregard any theory of morals in his search for truth. Beauty's world is remote from both these standards; she aims neither at morals nor at truth. Her imaginary creations, by definition, make no pretence to reality, and cannot be judged by reality's tests. The poet's only moral duty, as a poet, is to be true to his art, and to express his vision of reality as well as he can. If the ideals enunciated by poets are not those which we admire most, we must blame not the poets but ourselves: in the world where morals count we have failed to give them the proper material out of which to rear a nobler edifice. This is inherent in the nature of our common humanity, and is not affected by the special conditions of any single society in space and time: though art is a symbol of the eternal conflict between aspiration and reality, it must at the same time remain forever a symbol of mortal imperfection. Critics everywhere except in America have ceased to test literature by the standards of ethics, and recognise in art an inevitable expression of a side of man's nature that can find no other realisation except in it.

We have done with the confusion between the drama and the theatre which has permeated dramatic criticism for over half a century. The theory that the drama is not a creative art, but a mere product of the physical exigencies of the theatre, is as old as the sixteenth century. An Italian scholar of that age was the first to maintain that plays are intended to be acted on a stage, under certain restricted physical conditions, and before a large and heterogeneous crowd; dramatic performance has developed out of these conditions, and the test of its excellence is therefore the pleasure it gives to the mixed audience that supports it. This idea was taken hold of by some of the German romanticists, for the purpose of justifying the Shakespearean drama in its apparent divergence from the classical "rules." Shakespeare cannot be judged by the rules of the Greek theatre (so ran their argument), for the drama is an inevitable product of theatrical conditions; these conditions in Elizabethan England were not the same as those of Periclean Athens; and it is therefore absurd to judge Shakespeare's practice by that of Sophocles. Here at least the idea helped to bring Shakespeare home to many new hearts by ridding the age of mistaken prejudices, and served a useful purpose, as a specious argument may persuade men to contribute to a noble work, or a mad fanatic may rid the world of a tyrant. But with this achievement its usefulness but not its life was ended. It has been developed into a system, and become a dogma of dramatic critics; it is our contemporary equivalent for the "rules" of seventeenth-century pedantry. As a matter of fact, the dramatic artist is to be judged by no other standard than that applied to any other creative artist: what has he tried to express, and how has he expressed it? It is true that the theatre is not only an art but a business, and the so-called "success" of a play is of vital interest to the theatre in so far as it is a commercial undertaking. "The success may justify the playwright," said an old French critic, "but it may not be so easy to justify the success." The test of "success" is an economic test, and concerns not art or the criticism of art, but political economy. Valuable contributions to economic and social history have been made by students who have investigated the changing conditions of the theatre and the vicissitudes of taste on the part of theatrical audiences; but these have the same relation to Criticism, and to the drama as an art, that a history of the publisher's trade and its influence on the personal fortunes of poets would bear to the history of poetry.

We have done with technique as separate from art. It has been pointed out that style cannot be disassociated from art; and the false air of science which the term "technique" seems to possess should not blind us to the fact that it too involves the same error. "Technique is really personality; that is the reason why the artist cannot teach it, why the pupil cannot learn it, and why the aesthetic critic can understand it," says Oscar Wilde, in a dialogue on "The Critic as Artist," which, amid much perversity and paradox, is illumined by some flashes of real insight. The technique of poetry cannot be separated from its inner nature. Versification cannot be studied by itself, except loosely and for convenience; it remains always an inherent quality of the single poem. No two poets ever write in the same metre. Milton's line:—

"These my sky-robes spun out of Iris' woof"

is called an iambic pentameter; but it is not true that artistically it has something in common with every other line possessing the same succession of syllables and accents; in this sense it is not an iambic pentameter; it is only one thing; it is the line:—

"These my sky-robes spun out of Iris' woof."

32

The New Criticism

We have done with the history and criticism of poetic themes. It is possible to speak loosely of the handling of such a theme as Prometheus by Aeschylus and by Shelley, of the story of Francesca da Rimini by Dante, Stephen Phillips, and D'Annunzio, or the story of King Arthur by Malory and Tennyson; but strictly speaking, they are not employing the same theme at all. Each artist is expressing a certain material and labelling it with an historic name. For Shelley Prometheus is only a label; he is expressing his artistic conception of life, not the history of a Greek Titan. It is the vital flame he has breathed into his work that makes it what it is, and with this vital flame (and not with labels) the critic should concern himself in the works of poets. The same answer must be given to those critics who insist on the use of contemporary material in poetry, and praise the poets whose subjects are drawn from the life of our own time. But even if it were possible for critics to determine in advance the subject-matter of poetry or to impose subjects on poets, how can a poet deal with anything but contemporary material? How can a twentieth-century poet, even when he imagines that he is concerned with Greek or Egyptian life, deal with any subject but the life of his own time, except in the most external and superficial detail? Cynics have said since the first outpourings of men's hearts, "There is nothing new in art; there are no new subjects." But the very reverse is true. There are no old subjects; every subject is new as soon as it has been transformed by the imagination of the poet.

We have done with the race, the time, the environment of a poet's work as an element in Criticism. To study these phases of a work of art is to treat it as an historic or social document, and the result is a contribution to the history of culture or civilisation, with only a subsidiary interest for the history of art. We are not here concerned with the value of such studies as empirical preparations or concomitants, but only in their relation to the essential and inherent nature of the critical act. "Granted the times, the environment, the race, the passions of the poet, what has he done with his materials, how has he converted poetry out of reality?" To answer this question of Francesco de Sanctis as it refers to each single work of art is to perform what is truly the critic's vital function; this is to interpret "expression" in its rightful sense, and to liberate Criticism from the vassalage to *Kulturgeschichte* imposed on it by the school of Taine.

We have done with the "evolution" of literature. The concept of progress was first applied to literature in the seventeenth century, but at the very outset Pascal pointed out that a distinction must here be made between science and art; that science advances by accumulation of knowledge, while the changes of art cannot be reduced to any theory of progress. As a matter of fact, the theory involves the ranking of poets according to some arbitrary conception of their value; and the ranking of writers in order of merit has become obsolete, except in the "hundred best books" of the last decade and the "five-foot shelves" of yesterday. The later nineteenth century gave a new air of verisimilitude to this old theory by borrowing the term "evolution" from science; but this too involves a fundamental misconception of the free and original movement of art. A similar misconception is involved in the study of the "origins" of art; for art has no origin separate from man's life.

"In climes beyond the solar road,
  Where shaggy forms o'er ice-built mountains roam,
  The Muse has broke the twilight-gloom";

but though she wore savage raiment, she was no less the Muse. Art is simple at times, complex at others, but it is always art. The simple art of early times may be studied with profit; but the researches of anthropology have no vital significance for Criticism, unless the anthropologist studies the simplest forms of art in the same spirit as its highest; that is, unless the anthropologist is an aesthetic critic.

Finally, we have done with the old rupture between genius and taste. When Criticism first propounded as its real concern the oft-repeated question: "What has the poet tried to express and how has he expressed it?" Criticism prescribed for itself the only possible method. How can the critic answer this question without becoming (if only for a moment of supreme power) at one with the creator? That is to say, taste must reproduce the work of art within itself in order to understand and judge it; and at that moment aesthetic judgment becomes nothing more nor less than creative art itself. The identity of genius and taste is the final achievement of modern thought on the subject of art, and it means that, in one of their most significant moments, the creative and the critical instincts are one and the same. From Goethe to Carlyle, from Carlyle to Arnold, from Arnold to Symons, there has been much talk of the "creative function" of Criticism. For each of these men the phrase held a different content; for Arnold it meant merely that Criticism creates the intellectual atmosphere of the age,—a social function of high importance, perhaps, yet wholly independent of aesthetic significance. But the ultimate truth toward which these men were tending was more radical than that, and plays havoc with all the old platitudes about the sterility of taste. Criticism at last can free itself of its age-long self-contempt, now that it may realise that aesthetic judgment and artistic creation are instinct with the same vital life. This relationship does not sum up the whole life of the complex and difficult art of Criticism, and does not imply that Criticism and creation are without profound differences; but it is this relationship which has been lost sight of and needs most emphasis now, for without it Criticism would really be impossible. "Genius is to aesthetics what the ego is to philosophy, the only supreme and absolute reality," said Schelling; and without subduing the mind to this transcendental system, it remains true that what must always be inexplicable to mere reflection is just what gives power to poetry; that intellectual curiosity may amuse itself by asking its little questions of the silent sons of light, but they vouchsafe no answer to art's pale shadow, thought; the gods are kind if they give up their secret in another work of art, the art of Criticism, that serves as some sort of mirror to the art of literature, only because in their flashes of insight taste and genius are one.

Prose and Verse

NOTHING could more completely prove the poverty of American criticism, its dependence on the decayed and genteel traditions of Victorian England, and its hopeless chaos in the face of new realities of art, than the recent discussions of the freer forms of verse. Both the friends and the enemies of *vers libres* have confined themselves within the limits of this narrow tradition; and the loudest advocates of modernity have defended their taste with the same stale platitudes as its foes. It is only because criticism always follows in this timid and halting way the new paths marked by the footsteps of poets, that we need not assume it to be a national trait rather than a universal failing.

It would be useless to take cognisance of all these outworn arguments, or to concern ourselves with the merely external history of these freer forms, from the days when Commodianus was accused of playing havoc with the traditional music of the Latin hexameter. But one of the most extraneous arguments must be dismissed at the outset. The admirers of *vers libres* have praised them because they are "democratic," while some of their enemies have actually found fault with them because they are "undemocratic," because they lack the regular beats which the true poetry of the people has always employed for communal effort. But democracy is a political ideal, and since when has a political ideal acquired the right to be regarded as a touchstone for poets? Dante's Roman Imperialism, Shakespeare's aristocracy, Carducci's republicanism, Shelley's democracy, all prove that one political ideal is as good as another as material for poetry, and that the problem for criticism to attack is not the political ideals of the poet but the poetry which he has made out of them. To go still farther, and to make politics a touchstone of rhythm and metre, is to leave the world of criticism and to enter that of Alice in Wonderland, where we might expect the talent of a poet to be tested by his opinions on the canals in Mars, or by his ability to eat as many oysters as the Walrus and the Carpenter. Only in a world where commas are Buddhist and exclamation points Mohammedan will it be reasonable to ask whether iambs and trochees are democratic or the reverse. How can poetry, or any form in which it expresses itself, whose very right to existence depends on its life, its reality, its imaginative power, be judged by a mere abstraction? It is the ever recurring malady of critics,—to formulate new abstractions on the basis of a dead art, and to "wish them" on the artists of a day still living.

No, if we wish to understand the ever changing forms of art, we must subdue our minds to every new expression, before we can hope to rise above it, and explain, in ever new and changing syntheses, its real meaning and the secret of its power. The direction which this new synthesis must take in the case of *vers libres* may best be understood after analysing and explaining some older and outworn ones.

Over two thousand years ago the question of the relationship of poetry and prose was opened for discussion by the Greeks, and the problem, as they stated it, is still agitating the minds of men

41

today. The weightiest of Greek arguments amounts to this: that the test of poetry is not the use of prose or verse, but imaginative power, for if metre were the real test, a rhymed treatise on law or medicine would be poetry and a tragedy in prose would not. This is Aristotle's thesis, and no critic or thinker in these two thousand years has been able to reason it away. But neither Aristotle nor any of his successors through the centuries has ever doubted the separate existence of prose and verse; those who admit his argument and those who deny it alike agree in conceiving of prose and verse as separate and distinct entities, each with its own characteristics and its own life. Poetry and verse may or may not be identical terms for them, but for all of them prose and verse are different and distinct. But are prose and verse different and distinct? Modern thinking has something new to say on this subject, and something that leads us to a new attitude toward the whole question of versification.

It is always safest to attack a problem first on its most external and superficial side; and so we may begin by examining some examples of the in-

Prose and Verse

finite variety of rhythm in human speech. Here is
a couplet from Pope's early *Pastorals:*

> "Let vernal airs through osiers play,
> And Albion's cliffs resound the lay."

Regularity in rhythm could hardly go farther;
there is an almost mathematical succession of beats
or accents. But in these lines from a blank verse
play of Beaumont and Fletcher there is less regularity:

> "I'll look thee out a knight shall make thee a lady too,
> A lusty knight, and one that shall be ruled by thee;
> And add to these, I'll make 'em good. No mincing,
> No ducking out of nicety, good lady,
> But do it home."

We can follow the faint shadow of regular metre
through these lines, but they certainly do not
follow the accepted conception of blank verse. The
Spoon River Anthology goes a step farther:

> "Over and over they used to ask me,
> While buying the wine or the beer,
> In Peoria first, and later in Chicago,
> Denver, Frisco, New York, wherever I lived,
> How I happened to live the life,
> And what was the start of it."

Some haunting sense of metre is here too, not the regular succession of classical tradition, but still some pattern of music in the mind of the artist that we can search for and discover. Shall we say that there is no sense of regular rhythm, fainter but still present, in this passage from De Quincey's prose:

"The case / was the same / precisely / as when / Ricardo announced / beforehand / that we should neglect / the variations / in the value / of money. / What could be / the use / of stating / every / proposition / as to price / three times over; / first, / in the contingency / of money / remaining / stationary; / secondly, / in the contingency / of its rising; / thirdly, / in the contingency / of its falling? / Such / an eternal fugue / of iterations, / such / a Welsh triad of cases, / would treble / the labor / of writer / and reader, / without doing / the slightest / service / to either. / "

These four examples illustrate, as well perhaps as a thousand, the variations and gradations of rhythm used by men in expressing their thoughts. They differ in the *degree* of their regularity of rhythm, but there is no place where we can sharply divide them in respect to their essential nature, and say that here verse ends and here prose begins.

44

Prose and Verse

All we can say is that out of the infinite variations of rhythm, we may conveniently classify the
more irregular as prose and the more regular as
verse.

We may go still further and take two lines in
which two poets appear to aim at the same succession of beats or accents,—where they have apparently used the same "metre." Compare this line of
Shakespeare:

"In his study of imagination"

with this of Milton:

"Rocks, caves, lakes, fens, bogs, dens, and shades of
death."

In theory these lines conform to the same metrical
arrangement. Both are in blank verse, with the
same traditional succession of five accented feet;
yet who can fail to see that they differ from each
other as widely as Pope's verse from De Quincey's
prose? But we need not go to two different poets;
if we take any two succeeding lines from the same
poet, in the same poem, and in what would be con-
ventionally called the same metre, though the dif-

ference may not be so striking, we are forced to the same conclusion:

"Thy rare gold ring of verse (the poet praised)
Linking our England to his Italy."

So that not only is there no sharp line dividing prose and verse, but whatever distinction exists between words in metre and words without it exists in exactly the same way between verses written in the same metre.

But the problem is, after all, far more fundamental than that. It has been touched only on its most external, indeed on a wholly negligible, side, and the questions that go to the heart of the whole matter have not yet been asked: In what sense can we say that verses written in the same metre,—the four just quoted, or any others that might possibly be quoted,—have anything in common merely because there is a somewhat similar succession of syllables and accents? In what sense does this purely external resemblance help to explain their music, their meaning, or their power? When we are concerned with this external resemblance, however great we may admit the resemblance to be, are we not occupied with quite another problem than the one which is the real concern of criticism, the problem of the special and unique quality of a poet's work?

To answer these questions is to lift the discussion out of the arid field of versification into the realm where it rightly belongs, the realm of criticism and aesthetic thought. This is where the discussion has of late been lifted by a group of modern thinkers, and this is where it must hereafter remain. For they have made clear the fundamental distinction between the mechanical whirr of machinery, or the ticking of a clock, and the inner or spiritual rhythm of human speech. They have made clear that only physical things can be measured, and that what can be so measured in a poet's verse, or in any work of art, is without artistic value, and a matter of complete indifference for all true criticism. They have made it clear, in a word, that rhythm and metre must be regarded as aesthetically identical with style, as style is identical with artistic form, and form in its turn is the work of art in its spiritual and indivisible self. Only those who regard style, or form, as something that can be added to, or substracted from, a work of art, will ever again conceive of metre as something separate from the life of the poem itself, as a poet's dainty trills or *coloratura* instead of the music of his whole manner of being.

Yet poetry is not unlike all the other facts of life; it is possible to approach it from many angles, to study it from many points of view. You love a friend; you admire his charm of manner, his frankness or his courtesy, his honour or honesty, his intelligence, his taste, his buoyant spirits, his handsome face, even his glowing health; but ultimately you love him for the personality that makes him himself, the personality that is compounded of all these qualities yet is independent of them all. But you recognize that it is possible and proper to consider him in any one of these ways by itself, and even in others. He is a human being, and the anatomist or physiologist can tell you secrets of his bones and blood that are hidden from you. You do not doubt the value of anatomy or physiology, in its own field, when you say that it can tell you nothing to explain why you loved this particular friend so naturally and so well.

48

Poetry, too, can be studied as a dead thing no less than as a living and breathing power. The words and syllables of which it is compounded may be counted, tabulated, and analysed; the succession of its external accents may be enumerated and compared; the history of each word traced back to some ancient source. Etymology, versification, syntax are respectable sciences, and have their proper place in the wide field of human knowledge. They are the anatomy or physiology of poetry. But they do not help us to understand the secret of poetic power, for the simple reason that poetic power is independent of accidental and external resemblances. The fact that two lines have the same external succession of beats or accents, conform or do not conform to the same "metre," follow or do not follow some traditional system of versification, tells us no more about their intrinsic quality as poetry than the fact that two men have the same bones or the same lymphatic system tells us about their special qualities as statesmen, as friends, or as men.

What is true of metre is also aesthetically true of language itself. To speak of "learning a language" is to risk the danger of the same confusion, for we do not learn language, we learn how to create it. That is why it is so wide of the mark to explain English words in terms of their continental antecedents, or to justify modern slang on the ground of its similarity to some foreign or classical usage. It has recently been urged, for example, that "to sail into a man" is a vivid and powerful phrase, because (of all reasons!) the Latinism "to inveigh against a man" means the same thing. But the Latinism in this case helps to explain the English phrase as much as the disinterred skeleton of a thirteenth-century English yeoman helps to explain the personality of John Masefield. To deal with abstract classifications instead of artistic realities,—versification instead of poetry, grammar instead of language, technique instead of painting,—is to confuse form as concrete expression with form as an ornament or a dead husk.

The essential truth, then, is this,—that poets are forever creating new rhythms, not reproducing old ones, a feat only possible for the phonograph. It will always be convenient and proper to identify and classify the new rhythms by their superficial resemblance to the old ones; and so we shall continue to speak of "anapaests," "trochees," "heroic couplets," or "blank verse," at least until better terms are invented, just as we speak of tall men and short men, large books and small books, without assuming that the adjectives imply fundamental distinctions of quality or character. But a classification intended merely for convenience can never furnish a vital basis for criticism; and for criticism the question of versification, as something separate from the inner texture of poetry, simply does not exist. All we can say is that the mood of prose can never be the mood of poetry.

Dramatic Criticism and the Theatre

IN ONE of the largest American Universities there is a room filled with theatrical bric-à-brac which is called "The Dramatic Museum." Actors, theatrical managers, antiquarians, and millionaires have added to a collection begun by the University authorities; and the museum now contains reproductions of the great theatres of the ancient and modern world, masks, prompt-books, playbills, and all the other accessories of the stage. The room may or may not contain collections of plays (for I have never visited it); but in any event, they are subsidiary to the main object of the directors, which is to illustrate the changing conditions of the theatres of the world as an essential introduction to the study of the drama.

Now, there can be no legitimate objection to the study of theatrical antiquities as a thing in itself. Human curiosity finds a natural satisfaction in searching the past for every manifestation of man's activity and ingenuity; and who shall say that the antiquities of the theatre, that house of a thousand wonders, may not be studied with interest (and even with intelligence) by those who are especially attracted by the stage and its history? Manuscripts, parchments, missals, bindings, and typography are a legitimate object of study for both those who are interested and those who are not interested in the contents of books; and the history of the theatre may furnish amusement both to those who love the drama and to those who care nothing for what the drama really has to offer the souls of men. The professional printer may profitably spend his spare hours in studying the history of printing, without concerning himself with the literature which the printed page gave to the world; the actor may amuse himself intelligently by ransacking stage memoirs or studying theatrical antiquities, without adding to his knowledge of dramatic poetry; and who shall say them nay? Both printer and actor become students of *Kulturgeschichte* in the process, though, like Monsieur Jourdain, they may not know it; they are both exploring outlying regions in the field of human culture.

But the fact is that the collection in the American University has not been brought together for this reason. It has a far more pretentious purpose than this. It is called a "dramatic" (not merely a theatrical) museum, and those responsible for its existence have brought together their interesting collection because they believe that these theatrical antiquities are an essential instrument of dramatic criticism. They believe that dramatic literature cannot be intelligently studied without an understanding of all that has gone on in the playhouses of the world from the very beginnings of the drama. The shape of the stage, the scenery, the audience and its characteristics, the lighting of the house, and many other things must be considered and understood before the art of the drama can be understood and appreciated. This raises a serious question of literary theory. For while we were willing to follow the printer's studies in the history of typography, with real interest, and without a careful weighing of the relative merits of printing and other arts and crafts, the case would be quite different if he insisted that we cannot understand the history of literature without studying the history of printing; and we should be especially inclined to examine the merits of his contention if we found that it was accepted without question by a considerable number of literary critics. The thesis of the directors of the "dramatic museum" is a popular one in this age; actors, playwrights, and dramatic critics alike agree with them. What is the history of this thesis, and what are its merits? What authority in the past has this theory that the criticism of dramatic literature must rest on a knowledge of the conditions of the theatre, and how weighty and convincing does this authority appear? These are the questions which this essay attempts to answer.

It is obvious at the outset that we shall not have to concern ourselves with the general effect of acting or representation on a dramatic work. That professional actors may interpret plays with verve and power and insight beyond the skill of men unaccustomed to visualise or portray human passion and human action; that the actor's art may in a sense vitalise the written word and give it a new magic; that the theatre may add a new and wonderful sensuous beauty to the imagination of the poet,—these are statements which it is wholly unnecessary to contest. So when Voltaire, dedicating his tragedy of *Zulime* to a popular actress of his time, tells her that "without great actors, a play is without life; it is you who give it its soul; tragedy is intended to be acted even more than to be read," he is stating an opinion which is beyond the scope of this discussion. It would be a simple matter to collect, from dedications and prologues and prefaces, from Marston's *Malcontent* and Webster's *Devil's Law Case* to the published plays of our own day, the *obiter dicta* of practical playwrights who have expressed themselves as dissatisfied with the printed page as the sole or the final medium of expression for dramatic writing. We need not be greatly impressed by these casual and uncritical utterances, which tell us nothing of the creative act that produced the work of art, but merely echo the ambitions which the artist cherishes for the children of his brain before or after they are born. They do not differ fundamentally from the whim of a poet who might maintain that his verses could not be thoroughly appreciated unless they were printed on vellum, in beautiful type, and with wide margins. But utterances of this kind do not concern us here; for the idea in which for the moment we have a special interest is that the theatre and the drama are not two distinct things, but only one; that the actor and the theatre do not merely externalise the drama, or interpret it, or heighten its effect, but that they *are* the drama; that the drama, in a word, is not so much a creative art born in the brain of the playwright as an historic product shaped by theatres and actors, and therefore not to be understood or studied without reference to them.

Even in this form we find the problem propounded at the very beginnings of dramatic criticism. Aristotle, in the fourth chapter of the *Poetics*, makes a distinction between the consideration of tragedy in itself and its consideration with reference to theatrical representation; but the text of the passage is so corrupt and confusing that it is hardly possible to found a theory, or even shape a clear antithesis, on the basis of this utterance. In several other passages, however, he has clearly enough stated his point of view. Tragedy, he tells us, has six parts, plot, character, diction, thought,

song, and scenery. By the last is meant the spectacle presented by the play upon the stage, the
scenery, the *mise en scène*, or perhaps merely the
actors in their tragic costume; but at all events the
purely theatrical side of a drama. This, he says in
the sixth chapter,

"has an emotional attraction of its own, but of all the
parts it is the least artistic and connected least with the
art of poetry. For the power of tragedy, we may be
sure, is felt even apart from representation and actors.
Besides, the production of spectacular effects depends
more on the art of the stage machinist than on that of
the poet."

This statement is repeated and reinforced with
argument throughout the *Poetics:*—in the seventh
chapter, where we are told that the length of a
play must be determined by an inner need, for

"the limit of length in relation to dramatic competition
and sensuous presentment is no part of artistic theory";

in the fourteenth chapter, where there is a contrast between the superior poet who arouses tragic
pity and fear by means of the inner structure of
the piece, and the inferior poet who does so by
means of the external spectacle of the theatre:

"for the plot ought to be so constructed that, even without the aid of the eye, he who hears the tale told will thrill with horror and melt with pity at what takes place";

and finally in the twenty-sixth chapter, where Aristotle sharply distinguishes between the poetic and histrionic arts, and tells us that

"tragedy, like epic poetry, produces its true effect even without action; it reveals its power by mere reading."

Casual references to the part played by actors and the theatre in the make-up of a play may mislead moderns into thinking that Aristotle is not wholly consistent in this matter. But the fact is that he cannot help thinking of plays in connection with their theatrical representation, any more than most of us can think of men and women without clothes. They belong together by long habit and use; they help each other to be what we commonly think them. But he does not make them identical or mutually inclusive. A play is a creative work of the imagination, and must be considered as such always, and as such only.

From the later Italian Renaissance to the end of the eighteenth century, the *Poetics* found scores, indeed hundreds, of translators and commentators throughout Europe; and Aristotle's position was tamely accepted by virtually every one of them. That this should be so in the Italy of the sixteenth century need excite no wonder, since the traditions of the theatre were still to be created for modern Europe. But in the next century we find even Corneille, in his three *Discours,* dismissing the whole subject of stage decoration and scenery, because Aristotle said they do not properly concern the poet; and this despite his own complaint that most dramatic critics have discussed the drama as philosophers and grammarians wholly lacking in all experience of the theatre. So Dryden, true to the ideals of his master Corneille, tells us that it is his ambition as a playwright to be *read:* "that, I am sure, is the more lasting and the nobler design." So the great French scholar, Dacier, at the end of the seventeenth century, admits that while stage decoration adds to the beauty of a play, it makes the piece in itself neither better nor worse; and yet he feels that it is valuable for the poet to understand the theatre, in order that he may know whether his play is well acted and whether the scenery is proper to the piece. So in the middle of the next century, Voltaire, in the notes to the tragedy of *Olympie,* says:

"What has the stage decoration to do with the merit of a poem? If the success depends on what strikes the eyes, we might as well have moving pictures!"

And so at the end of the same century, the poet laureate Pye, if we may dare to disinter his work in the face of Byron's and the world's contempt, says in his commentary on the *Poetics:*

"There are few good tragedies in which the effect is not in general at least as forcible in the closet as on the stage, even in the modern theatre. In the strongly impassioned parts, where every other consideration of effect is lost in feeling, we are wonderfully moved by the natural efforts of a Garrick or a Siddons; but this is independent of the stage effect, and would be as strong in a room as on the stage."

The first to challenge this theory of the drama was a scholar and critic of the later Renaissance, Lodovico Castelvetro, who published an Italian version of Aristotle's *Poetics* in 1570. The version is embedded, one might almost say lost, in an elaborate commentary of over three hundred thousand words, which covers the whole field of literary theory with remarkable thoroughness and with even more remarkable independence of mind. Indeed, this independence of mind gained for him the rancor of classicists in all the countries of Europe for a century or more, and several pages might be filled with the protests of continental scholars and critics against what seemed to them the perversity, the heretical doctrines, and the excessive subtlety and acuteness of Castelvetro's book. He was an aggressive controversialist by temperament, belonging to those "literary gladiators of the Renaissance" (as Nisard calls them) who regarded scholarship as an instrument of logical disputation as much as (if not more than) a means of uncovering buried truth. It is easy for any shallowpate to disagree with Aristotle now; but when we consider that the theory of Aristotelian infallibility in letters died hard even at the end of the eighteenth century, and that even Lessing thought the *Poetics* as infallible in criticism as Euclid in geometry, we must salute the commentator who did not fear to take direct issue with Aristotle at the end of the sixteenth century.

Dramatic Criticism

Castelvetro certainly takes issue with Aristotle on the question whether the drama exhibits its real power in the study or in the theatre. "Non è vero quello che Aristotele dice," he says: it simply is not true, what Aristotle says, that the value of a play can be discovered by reading in the same way as by theatrical representation, for the reason that a few highly gifted and imaginative men might be able to judge a play in this way, whereas every one, the gifted and the ignorant alike, can follow and appreciate a play when it is acted. Nor is it true, he tells us elsewhere, that the same pleasure is derived from the reading of plays as from seeing them on the stage; the pleasure is different in kind, and the peculiar pleasure of a play is to be derived only from its representation in the theatre. In order to understand what the drama is, and what is the peculiar pleasure that it affords to men, we must examine the conditions of the physical theatre, and realise exactly what is to be found there. The fact that the drama is intended for the stage, that it is to be acted, must form the basis of every true theory of tragedy or comedy.

A number of years ago I pointed out Castelvetro's priority in stating this theory of the theatre, and I can only repeat the summary that I gave of it then. What, according to him, are the conditions of stage representation? The theatre is a public place, in which a play is presented before a motley crowd—*la moltitudine rozza*—upon a circumscribed platform or stage, within a limited space of time. To this idea the whole of Castelvetro's dramatic system is conformed. In the first place, since the audience may be great in number, the theatre must be large, and yet the audience must be able to hear the play; hence verse is added, not merely as a delightful accompaniment, but also in order that the actors may raise their voices without inconvenience and without loss of dignity. In the second place, the audience is not a select gathering of choice spirits, but a motley crowd of people, drawn to the theatre for the purpose of pleasure or recreation; accordingly, abstruse themes, and in fact all technical discussions, must be avoided by the playwright, who is limited, as we should say today, to the elemental passions and interests of men. In the third place, the actors are required to move about on a raised and narrow platform; and this is the reason why deeds of violence, and many other things which cannot be acted on such a platform with convenience and dignity, should not be represented in the drama. And finally, the physical convenience of the people in the audience, who cannot comfortably remain in the theatre without food and other physical necessities for an indefinite period of time, limits the length of the play to about three or four hours.

Many of Castelvetro's incidental conclusions may seem hopelessly outworn today; but the modernity of his system is self-evident, if by modernity we mean agreement with the theories that happen to be most popular in our own time. Certainly, for nearly two centuries, the path which he blazed was not crowded with followers. A few writers during the seventeenth and eighteenth centuries, a very few, echo haltingly and intermittently some of his ideas about the relations of the drama and the actual theatre. But it was not until the days of Diderot that they found again systematic and intelligent discussion. In several of Diderot's essays and dialogues,—in his discourse on dramatic poetry, in his famous *Paradox of the Actor*, but more especially in his *Entretiens sur le Fils Naturel*,—the accents of "modernity" are even more apparent than in his Italian predecessor, and one or two notes are sounded that are so much of our own time that it seems difficult to believe they can be older than yesterday.

Diderot's central idea in the *Entretiens* is that the essential part of a play is not created by the poet at all, but by the actor. Gestures, inarticulate cries, facial expressions, movements of the body, a few monosyllables which escape from the lips at intervals are what really move us in the theatre; and to such an extent is this true, that all that really belongs to the poet is the scenario, while words, even ideas and scenes, might be left to the actor to omit, add to, or alter. He himself sketches the scenario of a tragedy in monosyllables, with an exclamation here, the commencement of a phrase there, scarcely ever a consecutive discourse. "There is true tragedy," he cries; "but for works of this kind we need authors, actors, a theatre, and perhaps a whole people!"

Yes, obviously actors, even authors, but why a

theatre and a whole people for drama like this?
Because the mere presence of a large number of
people assembled together in a theatre has its own
special effect that must be considered in every
discussion of the drama. Here we meet, although
not for the first time, what is now known as the
theory of the "psychology of the crowd." Bacon,
in the *De Augmentis*, had pointed out the wonderful effectiveness of the theatre as an instrument of public morality, in the hands of ancient
playwrights, and explained this effectiveness on
the ground that it is a "secret of nature" that men's
minds are more open to passions and impressions
"congregate than solitary." Before him Castelvetro
had estimated the influence of the theatrical audience in general on the nature of the drama, finding
it especially in the necessity imposed upon the
playwright of avoiding all themes and ideas un-
intelligible to the miscellaneous gathering at a
theatrical performance. But Diderot finds a dual
effect. Mobs and popular revolts make it clear how
contagious is passion or excitement in a great con-
course of people; self-restraint and decency have
no meaning for thousands gathered together,

whatever may be the temperament of each individual in the crowd. The effect of the play is heightened for each spectator because there are many spectators to hear and see it together; but the presence of the crowd has a kindred influence on the playwright and the actor. They, too, share the effect of the "psychology of the crowd:" the actor has the crowd before him in fact, the poet in imagination, and both do their work differently than if they were preparing a solitary entertainment. Like the orator on the public platform or the mountebank on the street corner, the playwright must suit his particular audience or he will fail.

This, says Diderot, is the secret of the failure of French tragedy in the eighteenth century. The Greek drama is the product of a vast amphitheatre, the enormous crowds that frequented it, and the solemn occasions that brought them together; these explain its simplicity of plot, its versification, its dignity and emphasis, all proclaiming a discourse chanted in spacious places and in noble surroundings. The French drama, however, has imitated the emphasis, the versification, the dig-

nity of the Greeks, but without the physical surroundings that made the ancient drama suited to
its environment, and without the simplicity of plot
and thought that its other methods justify. Sim-
plify the French play and beautify the French
stage: this is Diderot's recipe for restoring the
glory of Greek drama in the modern world; a
larger and more adequate theatre and more beautiful stage decoration are the first prerequisites of
reform. It is Voltaire's recipe too: the elimination
of petty gallantry from the French drama and the
substitution of an adequate edifice for the "narrow
miserable theatre with its poor scenery."

The world will never cease to seek external
cures for inner deficiencies of the human spirit;
and yet every age must protest against this form
of quackery in its own way. In this case it was
left to Lessing to point out Diderot's and Voltaire's more obvious errors. Lessing's *Hambur-
gische Dramaturgie* was a product of actual contact
with the theatre; it is, at least apparently, a discussion of one play after another as Lessing saw
them acted on the stage. But out of this accidental
succession of theatrical performances he formu-

lates a more or less consistent programme for the development of a new and more vital dramatic literature in his own country; not, however, by means of an improved theatre or more elaborate stage decorations, but by a new and creative impulse in the plays themselves. In the eightieth number of the *Dramaturgie* he answers the theatrical arguments of Voltaire and Diderot by an appeal to history. The Shakespearean drama, considered in connection with the poverty of Elizabethan stage decoration, proves conclusively for him that there is no real relation between elaborate scenery or splendid theatrical edifices and great drama itself. Does every tragedy need pomp and display, or should the poet arrange his play so that it will produce its effect without these external aids? Lessing's answer to these questions is identical with Aristotle's. Indeed, he forestalls Lamb's theory that a great play cannot be properly acted at all: "A masterpiece is rarely as well represented as it is written; mediocrity always fares better with the actors."

Still there must lurk a doubt in regard to his consistency. "To what end the hard work of the dramatic form?" he asks; "Why build a theatre, disguise men and women, torture their memories, invite the whole town to assemble at one place, if I intend to produce nothing more with my work and its representation than some of those emotions that would be produced by any good story that every one could read by his chimney-corner at home?" We may well ask ourselves what Lessing really means by this question. There never was a thing written, lyric, ballad, epic, drama, or what not, that was not strengthened in the impression it makes, by having a noble voice or an exquisite art express it for us. Of course the trained actor gives a new fire and flavour to the drama; of course attendance at a theatre adds pleasures to those derived merely by reading a play in solitude; of course when we have recourse to sound and sight, to music and architecture and painting, in the theatre, we are adding complicated sensations to those that properly spring from the nature of the drama itself. If Lessing means to ask whether these added sensations are worth the cost of building theatres and training actors, who will answer no? But if he means to imply that it would not

be worth building theatres and training actors unless the drama were a *vie manquée* without them,
then we can only answer his question by asking
some of our own. Why build libraries, train li-
brarians, perfect systems of library administration
and bibliography, if we get nothing out of a book
in a library that we could not get out of it in our
study at home? Why develop the arts of typography and binding, if we can get as.much pleasure
out of a volume in manuscript as out of a printed
book; or why have beautiful type and rich bindings, if we can find the real soul of a book in the
cheapest and ugliest of types and bindings? These
questions bring with them their own *reductio ad
absurdum;* for obviously we build libraries, and
develop the arts of typography and binding, for
quite other reasons than that books are not books
without them, or that the critic must consider any
of the three when he is criticising the content of a
book.

Forty years of historical research, of aesthetic
theory, and of wider acquaintance with the literatures of the world intervened between the *Ham-
burgische Dramaturgie* and Schlegel's *Lectures on*

Dramatic Art and Literature; and in these the
methods inaugurated by Castelvetro were applied,
if not for the first time, at least with the largest
amount of consistency, to the actual history of the
drama. In Schlegel's first two lectures we find all
the theories we have already met, as well as others
of kindred intention. The drama is dialogue, but
dialogue with conflict and change, and without personal explanation of this conflict or change on the
part of the playwright. There is only one way in
which this can be done: by having men and women
actually represent the characters, imitate their
voices and temperaments, and carry on the discourse in surroundings that have some similarity
to those imagined by the playwright. Without this
help (and this is Schlegel's central idea) dramatic
dialogue would demand personal explanation on
the part of the playwright to make his meaning
clear; that is forbidden by the very idea of drama;
and so the theatre is implicit in the nature of drama
itself. In the theatre, "where the magic of many
combined arts can be displayed," these all help
the playwright in "producing an impression on an
assembled multitude." Here we are once more

faced by the theory of the "psychology of the crowd." According to Schlegel, the main object of the drama is to "produce an impression on an assembled crowd, to gain their attention, and to excite in them interest and participation." The impression is intensified by reason of the numbers that share it: "The effect produced by seeing a number of others share in the same emotions . . . is astonishingly powerful."

For Schlegel, the theatrical and the dramatic are bound together, not only in their very nature, but, as a consequence, in their history. Acting and theatrical performances of greater or lesser complexity are to be found in various primitive ages and among various primitive peoples, and mimicry is innate in man's nature. On these assumptions Schlegel sketches the earlier history of the stage, as indeed Aristotle had done for Greek tragedy, and carries on this history throughout his discussion of the modern drama. The Elizabethan theatre's paucity of stage scenery is cited as proof of the glory of Shakespeare, inasmuch as he was able to give the air of reality, to produce complete illusion, without such adventitious aid. And so

Schlegel proceeds in the case of each period of dramatic poetry; indicating the condition of the theatre almost always, but never quite arriving at the more modern conception by which the shape of the theatre or of the stage is regarded as having actually determined the nature of the drama in each age.

The Austrian playwright, Grillparzer, whose prose works abound in critical acuteness, came to regard Schlegel's lectures as "dangerous;" but the ideas they contained, so far as the relations of drama and theatre are concerned, had a germinal influence on his own dramatic criticism. He was the most aggressive opponent of the "closet-drama" that had yet appeared; and he was relentless in his contempt for all fine writing, soliloquies, and mere poetry that do not contribute to the "action" of a play. He goes so far as to say that the distinction between theatrical and dramatic is false; whatever is one must inevitably be the other. If time and space permitted, it would be interesting to discuss in detail Grillparzer's theories of the drama, especially as they have been neglected by English critics. But the fact is that intellectual hegemony in these matters had already passed to France while Grillparzer was still writing, and we cannot remain longer in the company of German theorists, although many of them have contributed largely, if not always wisely, to the subject under discussion.

There still remains one period of dramatic theory to consider, the period of theatricalism rampant. The French have been the masters of this form of dramatic criticism, and since the middle of the nineteenth century their footsteps have been followed with little or no protest by the critics of the world. Critics like Mr. A. B. Walkley and Mr. William Archer, not to mention their noisy but negligible echoes in our own country, have little enough to add to what Frenchmen had already said before them on this subject. The extremist in this movement, and indeed in some senses a pioneer, is Francisque Sarcey; and no one has gone further in the direction of making drama and theatre mutually interchangeable terms than he. Doubtless it was of him and his kind that Flaubert was thinking when he wrote to George Sand over forty years ago: "One of the most comical things of our time is this newfangled theatrical mystery (*l'arcane théâtral*). They tell us that the art of the theatre is beyond the limits of human intelligence, and that it is a mystery reserved for men who write like cab-drivers. The question of success surpasses all others. It is the school of demoralisation." Two years after this was written Sarcey summed up his code *in extenso* in an *Essai d'une Esthétique de Théâtre,* which still remains the clearest and most extreme expression of this form of dramatic materialism.

Sarcey assumes three fundamental hypotheses: first, that the only purpose of a play is to please a definite body of men and women assembled in a theatre; secondly, that in order to do this, the playwright is limited, or if you will, aided, by certain tricks and conventions of the theatre; and finally, some of these conventions change from age to age or from country to country, while others are inevitable and eternal. On the basis of these assumptions, he frames this pretty definition of the drama: "Dramatic art is the ensemble of conventions, universal or local, eternal or temporary, by the aid of which the playwright, representing human life in a theatre, gives to the audience an illusion of truth." *Voilà donc!* Here is the greatness of *Hamlet* and *Oedipus* most simply set down. Here is a definition that makes it an easy matter to understand the greatness of all the great plays of the past! Like nearly all his predecessors from the time of Castelvetro, of whom Sarcey had doubtless never heard, our aesthetician of the theatre places the idea of an audience first. When you think of the theatre, he says, you think of the presence of the public; when you think of a play, you think in the same instant of the public come to hear it. You can omit every other requirement, but you cannot omit the audience. It is the inevitable, the fatal *sine qua non*. To it dramatic art must accommodate all its organs, and from it can be drawn, without a single exception, all the laws of the theatre.

This is Sarcey's fundamental condition in 1876; and it is still fundamental with most of the dramatic critics of today. Mr. Walkley, for instance, in a half-solemn, half-facetious review of my lecture on "The New Criticism" which he did me the honour to write for the London *Times* a few

years ago, asserts that the dramatic critic can only
appraise a play "by an evaluation of the aesthetic
pleasure received," and that in order to do this,
he must "take into account the peculiar conditions"
under which the dramatist works. These peculiar
conditions are of course the audience of Sarcey
(Mr. Walkley calls it the "peculiar psychology
of the crowd he is addressing") and Sarcey's conventions of the theatre (although Mr. Walkley
limits them to "the conformation of the stage").
The critic of the *Times* has studied and considered,
perhaps more carefully than any of his predecessors, the various vicissitudes of this "conformation
of the stage." I have no reason to doubt his authority in the field of stage history; but his authority
ceases in the field of aesthetic theory. A writer who
has sense enough to understand that the dramatic
critic must "sit tight" against the prejudices and
opinions of theatrical audiences, preserving at all
hazards his own judgment (I am paraphrasing a
lecture of Mr. Walkley on *Dramatic Criticism*),
and who in the very next breath tells us that the
playwright must be judged by his effect on "the
peculiar psychology of the crowd he is address-

ing," has evidently not mastered the elements of aesthetic logic. As for Francisque Sarcey, who is responsible for so much of this cheap materialism of contemporary dramatic criticism, he seems to me as shallow a dogmatist as ever wrote criticisms of plays for the press; and decent invective can hardly go farther than that.

Now, what is meant by this idea, by no means modern, but in our day more persistent than ever, that the peculiar characteristic of dramatic literature is that it is intended for an assembled crowd? Obviously not merely that men are more impressionable in crowds than when alone, and that the dramatist has an advantage over most other writers in that he may make his appeal to men when they are most impressionable. This may be Bacon's thought, but it is far from being Diderot's or Schlegel's or Mr. Walkley's. What these men assert is that the crowd is inherent in the very idea of a play, and that this crowd has a peculiar psychology different in kind from that of any individual composing it. Indeed, I believe I have read some flighty utterances of late to the effect that so far from remaining civilised beings, we all revert to our primitive savage state when we become part of a crowd, and that the drama must therefore always appeal to what is primitive and savage in our natures more than any other form of literature. Well, the fact is that all of us are primitive men in spots, and that the theatre may appeal to what is primitive in us if it chooses; but so does fire, so does shipwreck or drowning, whether we choose or not; and for that matter, to get as far from the crowd as possible, so does solitude. If anything is certain in regard to that strange creature man, it is that in solitudes, what we call civilisation is most likely to fall from him; and we might with at least equal truth argue that lyric or didactic poetry, intended to be read in the quiet of a man's study, must appeal to the most primitive instincts in him, and that therefore all lyric or didactic poetry must of necessity deal with more primitive and savage themes than any other forms of literature. But the inner logic of art is independent of these incidental and extraneous classifications of artistic form. All literature makes its appeal to the same spiritual side of man's nature, and the appeal is not altered by any abstract classification, lyric, didactic, dramatic, or what not, which has no higher function than convenience of discussion.

Not only is the crowd different from its constituent individualities, and more primitive in instinct than they (I am of course summarising the virtues of the imaginary crowd created by modern psychologists and dramatic critics), but it is also inattentive, engrossed in itself, difficult to interest, and the first object of the playwright must be to compel its attention. But the fact is that most men and women (whether in a crowd or by themselves) are without the faculty of intellectual concentration. Great art ignores this and other like frailties of men, in the theatre and out of it; while mediocre art focuses its attention on them, in the novel, in song, ballad, lyric, essay, no less than in drama. A great Italian critic, indeed one of the greatest critics of the modern world, Francesco de Sanctis, gave this famous advice to a young poet anxious to know how he could best serve the higher morals in poetry: "Don't think about morals; that is the best way of serving them in art." In much the same way, we might say to the playwright: "Don't think about your audience; that is the best way of serving it in the drama."

It will be remembered that Pye, in commenting on Aristotle, pointed out that Garrick or Siddons reciting a dramatic poem in a room might affect us with the same pleasure as if they were acting in the theatre. Now, if we do not prefer rather to err with Mr. Walkley than shine with Pye, we may go a step farther, and assume that the audience of Garrick or Siddons in that little room has been reduced to a single spectator. Will there be any diminution in the power of Garrick or Siddons over him because of the absence of a crowd? Or even assuming that Garrick or Siddons might find a stimulus to added passion in the presence of a large audience, or that our single auditor would feel stimulated also by the crowd in the theatre, how can we for a moment believe that the pleasure he receives in the room is different in its *nature* from the pleasure received from the recitation in the crowded theatre? So that even histrionic art, not to mention dramatic art, speaks with the same voice in solitude as in crowds; and all the more then will the drama itself, "even apart from representation and actors," as old Aristotle puts it, speak with its highest power to the imagination fitted to understand and receive it.

No, Mr. Walkley and Brunetière and others like them are right when they say that the dramatic critic must "sit tight" against the prejudices of the crowd, must preserve his own judgment; which is only another way of saying that a play must be judged by its effect on an individual temperament—individual, yet representative of our common human nature—and *not* by "the peculiar psychology of the crowd." But unfortunately the demoralisation which forty years ago Flaubert foresaw in all this *arcane théâtral*, all this pedantry of "dramatic technique," of "dramaturgic skill," of *scènes à faire*, of the conditions of the theatre, the influence of the audience, and the conformation of the stage, this demoralisation, I say, has overwhelmed the criticism of the drama. What the unities, decorum, *liaison des scènes*, and kindred petty limitations and restrictions were to dramatic theory in the seventeenth and eighteenth centuries, these things are to criticism in the nineteenth and twentieth. They constitute the new pedantry, against which all criticism, as well as all creative literature, must wage a battle for life.

How deeply this pedantry has permeated the criticism of our age becomes even more obvious when we examine the work of the "aesthetic" critics themselves. They cannot wholly subdue their minds to so mechanical a theory, but its phrases and formulae they repeat in a sort of parrot-like fashion, even when in the next breath their truer understanding of poetry makes them deny its truth. So Mr. Arthur Symons, for example, tells us that "a play is written to be acted, and it will not be literature merely because its sentences are nicely written; it will be literature, dramatic literature, if in addition to being nicely written, it has qualities which make a stage-play a good stage-play." And yet in the same book, dealing with a particular play, he says that "the piece was constructed entirely with a view to effectiveness, superficial effectiveness on the stage, and not according to the variable but quite capturable logic of human nature; . . . as a thing to be acted, not as life, not as drama." This final jumble may be capped by a sentence of Mr. Laurence Binyon's, which might well serve as a minute masterpiece of confused aesthetic thinking: "If poets mean to serve the stage, their dramas must be dramatic." What can this mean except that if poets wish to make the theatre successful, they must write plays that will make the theatre successful? Or if it does not mean that, what else can it mean that is not equally meaningless? But to serve the theatre in any practical sense is not an aesthetic aim, and can never be the aim of a poet; there is only one way in which he can serve it well, and that is to express the best there is in him, and that only. The answer to Mr. Symons at his worst may well come from Mr. Symons at his best. No one has expressed that answer more clearly than he: "To you, as to me, whatever has been beautifully wrought, by whatever craftsman, and in whatever manner of working, if only he has been true to himself, to his own way of realising the things he sees, that, to you as to me, is a work of art."

Regarding the theatre, therefore, not as a place of amusement (although in that too it has of course its justification as much as golf or tennis), not as a business undertaking (in which case we

Dramatic Criticism

should have to consider the box-office receipts as
the test of a play's excellence), not as an instrument of public morality (since our concern here
is not with ethics or sociology), but regarding it
solely as the home or the cradle of a great art,
what do we find its relations to dramatic criticism?
Merely this, that for criticism the theatre simply
does not exist. For criticism, a theatre means only
the appearance at any one time or in any one country of a "series of artistic souls." When these artistic souls appear, theatres will spring up like mush-
rooms to house them, and the humblest garret will
serve as an eyrie for their art. But all these external conditions are merely dead material which
has no aesthetic significance outside of the poet's
soul; and only in the poet's art should we seek to
find them.

No misconception of art is so persistent as this
confusion between inner impulse and outer influence. A poet, let us say, finds that a brisk walk
stimulates his writing, or that he can write more
easily when he has smoked a cigarette. The walk
or the cigarette has not produced the poetry; it
has simply served as a stimulus to the personality

that creates the poetry. It opens the faucet, but who would be so foolish as to maintain that it produces or alters the water that gushes forth? Other poets find that they cannot write easily without the stimulus of imagined reward,—money, the plaudits of the crowd, the resplendent beauty of theatrical performance. But men with the same ambitions write different poems or plays, and in this difference lies the real secret of art. For after all, whatever the imaginary stimulus, there is only one real urge in the poet's soul, to express what is in him, to body forth his own vision of reality as well as he can. To say, therefore, that playwrights write for the stage, that poets write for money, that painters paint to be "hung," is to confuse mere stimulus with creative impulse.

For Mr. William Archer this distinction, one of the most fundamental of all distinctions in criticism, is a mere dispute between Tweedledum and Tweedledee; and so it may well seem to a conventional mind, angered and confused by the thought of a new age that has become impatient at his commonplaces. For him the relation of the drama to the theatre is exactly the same as that of a ship to

the sea. A play is "a ship destined to be launched
in a given element, the theatre. Here," he adds,
"Mr. Spingarn will at once interrupt, and say that
many plays are not so destined." But Mr. Spingarn
says nothing of the kind. What he really says is
that, rightly considered, *no* plays are so destined.
Every poet in the world may or may not have
written poems for money; it is a problem for the
young and not too discreet tyro in the economic
interpretation of history; but what concern is it of
the critic? For him no poem is written for money.
When we find that Mr. Archer simply cannot understand what this means,—when we find that he
cannot comprehend the distinction between utility
and beauty, between stimulus and creative impulse,
between the mechanical science of ship-building
and the spiritual act of artistic creation,—what can
we say to him? What is it possible to say except
that such a critic needs, not refutation, but a new
education?

So after wandering through the centuries we re-
turn at last to the collection of theatrical antiquities
in the American University. What has aesthetic
speculation from Aristotle to Croce to tell us about

this so-called "dramatic museum"? Why, that it contains either too little or too much. Too much, from the standpoint of dramatic criticism, which is concerned with externals, including the theatre, only in so far as they appear in dramatic literature itself. Too little, from the standpoint of the history of culture, because the theatre is only one, and a very insignificant one, of all the influences that have gone to make up dramatic literature.

If we examine the life of any dramatist from Aeschylus to Andreyev, or any play from *Sakuntala* to the *Playboy of the Western World,* we shall find a thousand influences affecting in some measure the artist and his work. *Hamlet,* for instance, is the work of a man whose father (let us say) was a butcher, and whose mother a gentlewoman; obviously, to understand a man of this sort, we should study the effect of his early visits to the butcher's shop on his later work, the influence of gentle birth on character, and the general problem of heredity. Our dramatic museum will be incomplete unless it contain books covering all these topics. The play is written by an Englishman, and who can tell what influence this fact may have had on the nature of the play? Surely the museum should provide us with histories of England, Warwickshire, Stratford, London, and with every conceivable book on the life and habits of the English people. Hamlet is the son of a king, and we should, of course, understand the ideals of royalty and of government in general in order to appreciate the ideas influencing Shakespeare in writing the play; we need a whole library of political science. Moral ideas are discussed throughout the play; where did they come from? The museum should furnish us with a library on the history of ethics. Hamlet is rather coarse in his language to Ophelia, and in numerous other ways reflects the Renaissance conception of woman and the position of women; so we realise that our museum would be incomplete without a whole library on woman, on social usages and customs, on dress, and heaven only knows what else.

But why continue? If the museum wishes to furnish us with the external material which influenced dramatic literature, it should furnish us with all the books, all the men, all the things, that

have existed side by side with the drama from
the beginning of its history and before; for all of
these men, or books, or things may have had a
larger and deeper influence than the physical theatre. But this, after all, is a problem of the history
of culture and not of criticism. If we wish to understand dramatic literature itself, we must seek
understanding in the great plays and not in the
dead material out of which plays are made.

A collection of theatrical bric-à-brac may interest and enlighten many men,—actors, impresarios,
stage-managers, playwrights, antiquaries, dilettanti
of all sorts, even University teachers of dramatic
literature, and who shall say how many others?
This essay challenges, not the museum's usefulness, still less its right to existence, but only the
theory of which it is a concrete expression; and
from this point of view it may well serve another
useful purpose, of which its founders perhaps took
no thought,—as a sort of literary "chamber of
horrors," a permanent symbol of the false theories
which have encumbered the dramatic criticism of
our time. For the true dramatic critic will transfer
his interest from the drama itself to the "laws of

the theatre" or the "conditions of the theatre" only when the lover studies the "laws of love" and the "conditions of love" instead of his lady's beauty and his own soul.

Creative Connoisseurship

(Letter to an Artist on the International Exhibition, February, 1913)

"To enjoy is, as it were, to create; to understand is a form of equality, and the full use of taste is an act of genius."—John La Farge's *Considerations on Painting*.

THE opening night of the International Exhibition seemed to me one of the most exciting adventures I have experienced, and this sense of excitement was shared by almost every one who was present. It was not merely the stimulus of colour, or the riot of sensuous appeal, or the elation that is born of a successful venture, or the feeling that one had shared, however humbly, in an historical occasion. For my own part, and I can only speak for myself, what moved me so strongly was this: I felt for the first time that art was recapturing its own essential madness at last, and that the modern painter and sculptor had won for himself a title of courage that was lacking in all the other fields of art.

Creative Connoisseurship

For after all, though it needs repeating in every civilisation, madness and courage are the very life of all art. From the days of Plato and Aristotle, who both shared the Greek conception of genius as a form of madness, to the Elizabethan poet who said of Marlowe:

"For that fine madness still he did retain
Which rightly should possess a poet's brain";

and from the sturdy and robust Dryden, with his

"Great wits are sure to madness near allied,"

to the living poet who was my own teacher and who writes

"He ate the laurel and is mad,"

all who have given any real thought to art or beauty have recognised this essential truth,—seeing in the poet's "madness" not something for the physician to diagnose, but fancy's eternal contrast with the common sense of a practical world. "Sense, sense, nothing but sense!" cried the German poet; "as if poetry in contrast with prose were not always a kind of nonsense." The virtue of an industrial society is that it is always more or less sane. The virtue of all art is that it is always more or less mad. All the greater is our American need of art's tonic loveliness, and all the more difficult is it for us to recapture the inherent madness without which she cannot speak or breathe.

You, I know, will not confuse this theory of poetic madness, to which poets themselves have given their faith, with the pseudo-scientific theories, current not many years ago, which pictured poets as "degenerate," "neurotic," or "mentally unbalanced." You will not confuse spiritual exaltation with physical disease. For the madness of poets is nothing more or less than unhampered freedom of self-expression,—expression of the real self, and not of mere eccentricity or whim. Those of us for whom self-expression is checked by inner or outer inhibitions must always look with something of amazement at those who can and do express themselves freely. For us they must always seem "mad." To let one's self go—that is what art is always aiming at, and American art at this moment needs most of all. It is in this sense that America needs the tonic madness of poets.[1]

[1] This idea is profoundly Greek and classical, though the

Creative Connoisseurship

But here was the poet's madness, and here was
courage that did not fear to be mad. I confess that
when I left the exhibition my feeling was not

academic mind can never understand this Dionysiac side of the
Greek soul. It is hardly necessary to quote the famous passage
in the *Phaedrus* in which Plato distinguishes the two types of
madness, "one [the madman's] induced by human infirmity, the
other [the poet's] a divine release of the soul from custom and
convention"; throughout the whole of his life Plato reaffirmed
his theory of poetic inspiration or madness, in the *Ion*, the
Meno, the *Symposium*, and the *Laws*. A "divine release from
custom and convention," or "from established usage"—there
is no trace of the pseudoclassical "decorum" here. "Even Aristotle, who sometimes writes as if the faculty of the logician
were enough to construct a poem," as Butcher puts it in his
Aristotle's Theory of Poetry and Fine Art, "says 'poetry is
a thing inspired' . . . In another place [in Aristotle] we
read of a poet who never composed so well as when he was
in 'ecstasy' or delirium"; yes, even in the *Poetics* (to quote
Bywater's translation) Aristotle definitely says that "poetry
demands a man with a special gift for it or else one with a
touch of madness in him." Similar expressions may be found in
every period of Greek history, from Democritus of Abdera, the
older contemporary of Socrates, or even Pindar, a century
earlier, to Longinus and Athenaeus in late Hellenistic times.
Pindar did not think that poetic inspiration was inconsistent with
his own adherence to rigidly prescribed forms; so that we may
say that Goethe's "In der Beschränkung zeigt sich erst der
Meister" is no more truly Greek than Dryden's "Great wits are
sure to madness near allied." For the Greeks, on the whole,
realised that the poet has to be able to do two things, to let
himself go and to master himself, and that the second is artistically impotent without the first.

merely one of excitement, but mingled with it was a real depression at the thought that no other artists shared this courage of the painters of our time. How timid seemed our poetry and our drama and our prose fiction; how conventional and pusillanimous our literary and dramatic criticism; how faded, and academic, and anaemic every other form of artistic expression. But these painters and sculptors had really dared to express themselves. Wrong-headed, mistaken, capricious, some of them may be; but at least they have the *sine qua non* of art, the courage to express themselves without equivocating with their souls. Some of them may have forgotten that the imagination is governed by an inner logic of its own, and not by unreasonable caprice; but even caprice is better than stagnation, even caprice is better than the lifeless logic of the schools.

And this leads me to what is really the inspiring cause of this letter, to the question that must occur to every mind: What have the patrons of art, the great American collectors, who are the envy and target of the world, what have they done for this exhibition, or for the artists who give it its flavour and power, and especially for the younger American artists who had the imagination and skill to bring it together? Did the masters of our national sanity encourage any of this divine madness; did they grapple with the pioneer work that you men are doing; or have they preferred to make timid but solid investments in the art whose original madness has been tamed, and placed beyond all question, by time?

We have heard altogether too much of the service which has been rendered by these "fake Lorenzo de' Medicis" of our time. I am tired of hearing that they have despoiled Europe and Asia of their treasures, and have filled not only their own homes, but public museums and libraries, with models of older beauty. I have lived many hours in that Renaissance of which Lorenzo was one of the flowers; and when I come back to my own country I find nothing that gives me less hope for its future than these very patrons and collectors who would ape his glory. For the very essence of his power is hidden from them. The soul of his purpose is at war with theirs. Theirs is at bottom acquisitiveness, his at bottom creativeness. For (it cannot be repeated too often) to enjoy and understand a work of art is to own it, in the only sense in which art takes cognisance of ownership; there is no other way to possess it except to live again the vision which the artist creates. But under all the garments that hide their purpose and make it fair, the desire to "shop," the hunger for other forms of property beside real estate and stocks and bonds, remain their real and unmistakable motives. His motive was as different from theirs as the sexual passion, creating life even without knowing it, is different from the desire to own slaves.

For look at Lorenzo's palace. Political and financial intrigue as real as any in the offices of the "interests" was harboured there. But inside the same palace lived poets and scholars, philosophers and painters, architects and engineers. All the world knows his architect Brunelleschi, his philosophers Ficino and Landino, his poets Poliziano and Luigi Pulci, his scholars Pico della Mirandola and Barbaro, not to mention the horde of painters and craftsmen who haunted his city and his house. Poliziano, one of the loveliest of all Italian poets, seems almost the product of his patronage, if it is proper to speak of a beautiful flower as the "product" of the gardener who waters it and gives it a fruitful soil. *He* did not merely load his rooms with the dead weight of dead centuries; *he* created, and fostered creation in others. And yet this was a merchant prince, like our own merchant princes; the inheritor of no greater power than theirs, the holder of no official position in the State that the prestige of his family did not earn for itself in the democracy of Florence.

But where is Morgan's Poliziano, where is Widener's Ficino? Where are the poems they have themselves written, as Lorenzo wrote his own *Ambra*, his own lovely *Nencia da Barbarino?* Where are the pageants and dramas they have composed or fostered, where the popular Muse (out of the mouths of the very rabble) that they have encouraged and refined? Where are the painters and scholars, poets and philosophers, dreamers and craftsmen of all kinds, who haunt their houses in the real intimacy that the old Renaissance fostered between prince and genius? While the Medicis made all Florence fertile with artistic life, these Americans, these mimic Medicis,

—so full of a power that seems dynamic and creative in the field of action, so colourless and timid in the field of taste,—have merely hung cold treasures in coy corners of remote aloofness that are now their graves as well as their homes.

But connoisseurship has its living as well as its dead side. If we were merely concerned with a craft that, in the presence of beautiful pictures, asked nothing but their age, their genuineness, their previous ownership, the meaning of their symbols and signatures, we might dismiss it without ado from our thoughts. For these are all problems with little or no aesthetic significance, and it is on a wholly different side that connoisseurship may become in the true sense creative. The collector, the patron, the critic have their common meeting ground in the realm of taste. To understand and enjoy beauty is their common bond; to re-create in their own souls the artist's vision of reality is at once their triumph and their joy. If they really express their own taste, instead of aping the taste of others, the work they do may be said to be creative like the artist's. Only this creative flowering of their own personalities may be called taste in any real sense; only this creative taste has a value for themselves or others.

For after all, patrons and collectors, prizes and rewards, boards and foundations have no significance for the artist, but only for the society which they represent. For art is not a flower that needs only watering and a fruitful soil to make it flourish; the gardener's kindly help is just as likely to kill it as to give it a new vigour. The parable of the poet who withers in a gilded chamber is the perennial symbol of art. Nothing outside of it seems really to help or to hinder; out of its own life it musters the mysterious power that helps it to speak or to be silent. So it is for their own sake, and not for the artist's, that the patron and the collector should cultivate the madness of poets. They may enrich the life and culture of the society of which they are a part, even though they can render no service to art. This is true of democracies as well as aristocracies: whether the patrons and collectors be few or many, whether they be rich or poor, whether they belong to a narrow circle to which the countersign is an heirloom from the past or include the whole wide range of human life, the problem remains exactly the same. Sympathy for artistic expression, and the power to understand and enjoy it, are independent of government in its varying forms; they are spiritual realities, and live in a world in which political abstractions and administrative details are merely shadows. That is why the flowering of taste remains always a symbol of the higher life of every age and every civilisation.

So our patrons and collectors, our amateurs and dilettanti, and all who wish to share the artist's vision of reality, can do something for America, and still more for themselves, without waiting for tomorrow. They can attend the International Exhibition; they can learn its lessons and enjoy or buy its pictures. They can share the artist's "madness," if only for a few heightened moments, and by their oneness with him in spirit once more justify the essential equality of genius and taste. They can help to make collecting itself a creative art, instead of a miser's hoarding lust. It is a choice between artistic life and artistic stagnation or death; and if you and your colleagues had done nothing more than to make possible, for us today, this ideal of creative collecting, the time and energy and insight you have spent on this work would be more than worth while.

Part II
OTHER ESSAYS

The Younger Generation

A NEW MANIFESTO
(1922)

Youth has always been regarded both as a physical fact and as a spiritual state, but to-day it must almost be regarded as a form of disease. We all know what it means as a physical fact: growth, puberty, the first shave, wisdom teeth, and all those stigmata of the body which preserve their perennial charm for men and women. But the spiritual state is almost as easily recognisable. We recognise its more superficial meaning when we say that "a man is as old as he feels," or that Theodore Roosevelt was never old and Woodrow Wilson never young. But in a deeper sense there is an ideal element of our youth which we carry with us through life and which never becomes old. In this sense youth is as precious as our very life-blood, an eternal possession which can and must be preserved against all the assaults of time; for it is in this sense that we are all poets, in this sense that we are creators and lovers of art.

The poet ceases to be a poet pure and simple when he outlives this spiritual state of youth, for poetry by its very nature is youth, in this wholly unchronological sense, the carrying on of that fresh vision of life which all of us preserve through life in varying degrees. The *Divine Comedy* is a profound poem written by a man who was no longer physically young; but what makes it a poem and not a treatise on philosophy is that Dante has preserved this spiritual state of youth which we call art or imagination, and which he has matured and enriched by experience and reflection but has never outgrown. This is in fact the general fate of men, for youth grows slowly into a realisation of its own intrinsic wonders, and the great works of the imagination are seldom if ever created by men who are physically young. Yet art is youth, and thought maturity, even though there may be old men who are flighty and fanciful, and young men who are thoughtful and well-poised. Art is youth, and judgment is maturity; and this is why it is impossible to expect art from those who have passed out of the spiritual state of youth or criticism from those who have not attained the spiritual state of maturity.

This is the spiritual youth to which we are all born and which nourishes a part of our inner life so long as we do not let it die. Physical youth is a fragile and ephemeral thing, and this is the imperishable part of it. But what shall we say of those who think that the fragile and ephemeral moment of physical youth is everything, that it is not merely the whole of reality but the sole test of excellence? What shall we say of the fashionable theory of our day that all art and all wisdom are the products of physical youth, that nothing is good unless men now young have done it or like it, and that therefore the test of ideas is not truth or the test of art, excellence, but the only test of both is "modernity"? This is not the healthy exuberance of youth "feeling its oats," or that equally healthy mingling of disdain and respect which is the normal attitude of young men toward their elders in all ages. This is a form of disease—if not the disease of those unfortunates who imagine themselves Emperors of India or Queens of France, at all events a disease akin to that of the impotent for whom a constant and irritable sense of rebellion takes the place of achievement, or the disease of the intellectualist who strives to make up for his artistic emptiness by the purely intellectual creation of "new forms." In this sense it is a disease from which men have suffered at all times, but in the narrower sense, as an attribute and as a special theory of youth, it is a disease of our time, confined to a somewhat narrow and unorganised but very articulate group.

It is natural in an age like ours, which is giving itself up more and more to abstractions and classifications rather than realities, that the disease should take the form of dividing men according to another abstract classification. The phrase which this *morbus gallicus* has coined for its victims, *les jeunes* or "the younger generation," matches such popular formulae as "labour," "the proletariat," "the public," and "the consumer." Indeed, the group of *les jeunes* is as "age-conscious" as certain groups of workingmen are "class-conscious." The first group limits life in its totality to a brief period of time, while the second sums up the whole of man's spiritual nature in terms of the economic moment of the spirit; and both voluntarily isolate themselves from that profound unity of thought without which life cannot yield up its highest secrets or achieve its noblest aims.

We need not wonder that these Davids are determined to destroy that Goliath, the Past. Seldom has humanity been moved by so deep a sense of failure, and its weariness of the past is weariness at its inability to solve its own inner problems. But this is the last way in which it can hope to solve them. For there is no past except the past that we love or hate: this past really lives for us, whether we love it or hate it; the only past that does not exist for us at all is the past we have forgotten and neither hate nor love. But if it lives for us it is no longer a past but a present; and the larger that present, the larger will be our own lives. To deny it is to deny our very selves, where alone it has its being. To limit our knowledge of it is therefore to circumscribe not the past but the present, to limit life itself in its deepest and richest sense. To hate not the past or the present, but an abstraction of which we know nothing and which we vaguely label "the past," is to mistake windmills for giants, and to limit even the horizon of our hates. No, we are not solving any problems, but merely escaping from them, when with a single careless gesture we dismiss "the past," and espouse the vague shibboleth of "modernity." It is six hundred years since Dante died, and the *Divine Comedy* means more to us today than it did to Dante's contemporaries. It lives not because it was ever "modern," for it never was, but because it is a great poet's vision of the life of man—not a mere synthesis of the thought and culture of any single age, but ancient, mediaeval, and modern all in one. "To seek modernity in art is to seek modernity and not art." We sneer at the rich men who discuss pictures in terms of the money paid for them; but the test of chronology is no more artistic than the test of price.

The craving for "modernity" is the fruit of the spirit of revolt that has reigned in our literature for a dozen years. I myself foresaw and approved of the revolt, even before my manifesto on "The New Criticism" in 1910. Our problem was in a sense different from the general problems of European culture. It was necessary to destroy the academic dry rot that was undermining the creative and intellectual spirit of the nation. It was necessary to rid ourselves of the last remnant of the older American "moralism" in thought and taste and action. It was necessary to destroy, not discipline, character, morals, imagination, beauty, freedom, which are the groundworks of all that is noble in art as in life, but the sterile forms which were made to serve instead of these realities. Not by making a fetish of these dead forms can we breathe the breath of a new life into the soul of man, but only by ridding ourselves of their spiritual burden, so that the spirit of life may once more be unhampered in the search for truth and beauty. And now the day for Revolt is over. For the "dissociation of ideas" is only the first, the crudest, the easiest step in the solving of human problems. To destroy a Bastille is not to build a city; and we who have destroyed many Bastilles must now look to the men who can answer our new question: What city of the spirit shall we build, and how? Destructivism, or Revolt for Revolt's sake, is the excess that grows out of the need of destruction, as licence out of liberty or the puritanical out of the moral. And so those who saw and welcomed the moment for rebellion must now submit to the creative control of thought and faith.

For the "disease" of this small body of young men, this narrow group of *les jeunes*, is not an isolated thing. It is part of a long period of suffering through which the world has been going for a century or more, and of which the World War is a mere incident, though it may serve the unseeing as a climax and a symbol. This world-epidemic has no name, and I shall give it none; but call it, if you will, Materialism, though that term limits and misnames it; call it Romanticism, though that term limits and misconceives it still more. The very same urge that makes *les jeunes* test art by physical age makes materialists, under the name of empiricism, positivism, or naturalism, conceive of philosophy not as a self-creative and independent science, but as merely one, and a very subordinate one, among the empirical sciences. The same outlook accounts for the wide currency of Bergsonian intuitionalism, Freudian instinctivism, and a still cruder behaviourism, with their contempt for the claims of the intellect; the same outlook makes men drape religion in the empty trappings of sociology, or evolve a mild and material code of conduct after the fashion of Confucianism as a substitute for the infinite riches of thought and faith; the same outlook drives men to accept tamely the dry bones of political liberalism or radicalism as an interpretation of life in its totality. It is this philosophy of materialism which has made us believe that the whole of life can be summed up in some single side of life—the economic side, the physical side, the psychological side. It is this outlook that divides the world. For the distinction between radicals and conservatives is as old-fashioned as that between monarchists and republicans, nominalists and realists, Platonists and Aristotelians, Jacobins and Girondists. Beyond mere sects, beyond the political and economic divisions that blind unforeseeing eyes, there is a larger field of combat. There is only one real division today that has any reality, and that is the difference between the old-fashioned materialisms or dualisms and the new spirit which (if we wish a name) may be called a new idealism, but is the only true realism to which modern man has attained.

Americans have a very vague and very queer conception of the meaning of idealism. For them it serves to cover a multitude of men and a multitude of sins. Plato was an "idealist," Woodrow Wilson was an "idealist," a man who gives money to charitable causes is an "idealist." In fact, all Americans are "idealists." But the word means none of these things. Its meaning is simple. It divides those who seek truth inside the spirit of man from those who seek it outside. In a sense all philosophy is idealism, for even the materialist posits no concrete and individual kind of matter, but the idea of matter, an idea of the mind. But because he has not remained true to the category of his own intrinsic assumption he becomes the enemy of idealism; and its enemies include not only materialism, but common-sense dualism, which crudely and completely separates matter and mind, and even the incomplete and subjective form of idealism, a narrow introspection, which denies or loses touch with one side of the essential antithesis of theory and practice, of subject and object. For all true idealism rests on the assumption that inner and outer reality are indissolubly intertwined in the realm of the spirit; and only on the basis of what is inside us can we build up that creative energy of thought and faith which the world has lost, and with it its happiness.

The chief championship of this outlook on life passed for a brief moment to Italy, where there has been an outburst of modern idealism that can in a sense be compared with that which gave Kant and Hegel, Goethe and Schiller, to Germany, or if you will, that which gave Jesus to Judaea—for in his words, "The kingdom of God is within you," is hidden the seed of all modern thought. Who would attempt to naturalise on our own soil the whole of this or any other foreign philosophy? If for some years I urged that we in America should go to school, not in the real, but in this wholly ideal Italy, it was not because I dreamt that its thinkers had found the final solutions of the problems that haunt the minds of men, but because I hoped they might guide us to a new knowledge of the meaning of life which we could make our own. For if they could not give up eternal verities, they might teach us again the language of thought, which we have forgotten. In them I found, or seemed to find, ammunition with which to destroy decaying citadels as well as brick and stone with which to build new cities. Yet when I gave the work of one of these Italian idealists, Gentile's *Reform of Education*, to a young friend of mine, he said that he could hardly fix his mind on it because it contained a vocabulary which he had never learned or had forgotten. He was used to discussing art and philosophy in terms of that crude mixture of economic, political, biological, and psychological jargon which is the earmark of our old-fashioned naturalism—"radicalism," "liberalism," "socialism," "democracy," "repressions," "complexes," "social reform," "evolution," "heredity," "environment." But in this Italian work such words either did not appear or were given a subordinate place as belonging outside the realm of art or thought. To my young friend words like "art," "thought," "the spirit," "the spirituality of culture," "expression," "faith," "freedom," "subject and object," seemed vague and "unscientific." Man instinctively gropes for some anchor, for some guide to deeper realities, in a word, for some religion; and intelligent youth cannot accept religion in the crudest of all its forms, the blind, unreasoning faith of the scientist or the economic materialist in an inexorable external Nature, instead of sharing in the higher struggles with truth of the philosopher and the seer.

It would be absurd to deny the empirical value of such sciences as biology and chemistry, medicine and psychology; nothing is farther from my thought than to cast slurs at any of them, for I have reason, in common with all men, to be grateful to them all. They furnish, as it were, the spadework of civilisation, forever widening the channels through which the spirit of man surges. But whatever value they may have on the plane of our practical lives, they must be left behind when we enter the realm of spiritual values; on the ideal planes of art and thought they have no place. The scientist must leave behind him his professional outlook in the search for truth and beauty, as completely as the stockbroker must leave *his* behind in the search for religion. This is the lesson that young America must learn if it would free itself

from the bondage of its restless and homeless life.
It must learn once more to speak and to think in
terms of ideal values. It must acquire a new vocabulary, or, if you will, it must take those old
words that once meant so much to men and breathe
the breath of life into them—those words that are
empty for us only because *we* are empty of the
thought that should be poured into them. We can
acquire a new vocabulary only by acquiring a new
life.

The American Critic

WHEN I wrote the essays which were collected in a volume bearing the subtitle of "Essays on the Unity of Genius and Taste," the pedants and the professors were in the ascendant, and it seemed necessary to emphasize the side of criticism which was then in danger, the side that is closest to the art of the creator. But now the professors have been temporarily routed by the dilettanti, the amateurs, and the journalists, who treat a work of the imagination as if they were describing fireworks or a bullfight (to use a phrase of Zola's about Gautier); and so it is necessary now to insist on the discipline and illumination of knowledge and thought,—in other words, to write an "Essay on the Divergence of Criticism and Creation."

American criticism, like that of England, but to an even greater extent, suffers from a want of philosophic insight and precision. It has neither inherited nor created a tradition of aesthetic thought. Golden utterances there have been aplenty—ut-

terances wise, or acute, or daring enough to con-
found those who refuse to recognise the American
spirit except where they find a faded moralism,—
utterances that anticipate the most modern concepts
of criticism throughout the world. To this American ancestry of my own thought I "point with
pride." [1] How can we forget Jefferson's *literary*
Declaration of Independence, with its contempt
for "the artificial canons of criticism" and its insistence that the only test of literary excellence is
whether a work gives pleasure and is "animating,
interesting, attaching,"—even though the idea of
pleasure no longer sums up for us the whole spiritual world of art? How can we forget Poe's con-

[1] The excerpts that follow, and many others of a similar nature, were collected under the title of "Passages Illustrating the
Growth of an American Tradition of Criticism" and published
as an appendix to this article when it appeared in *Criticism in
America: Its Function and Status,* 1924, pages 321-330. The
quotation from Thomas Jefferson is from his letter to William
Wirt, November 12, 1816; Emerson's definition of criticism
will be found in his *Journals,* June 6, 1838; and the passages
from Margaret Fuller are from her *Papers on Literature and
Art,* 1846. These excerpts are intended to illustrate "the growth
of *an* American tradition of criticism;" the task of summing up
"*the* American tradition of criticism" I leave to the pontifical
imagination of others.

ception of poetry as "the rhythmical creation of beauty" and of beauty as having "no concern whatever either with Duty or with Truth;" or Emerson's kindred idea that beauty, no less than truth, is "an ultimate end," and his definition of criticism, with its striking challenge, "Here was a new mind, and it was welcome to a new style"? Margaret Fuller believed like Goethe that the best critics "enter into the nature of another being and judge his work by its own law, but having done so, having ascertained his design and the degree of his success in fulfilling it, they do also know how to put this aim in its place and how to judge its relations," and said of Lowell as a poet that "his interest in the moral questions of the day has supplied the want of vitality in himself;" and yet even Lowell, as a critic, has clearly defined "the difference between what appeals to our aesthetic or to our moral sense, between what is judged of by our taste or by our conscience." The author of our first formal treatise on aesthetics, Moffat's *Introduction to the Study of Aesthetics,* published before the Civil War, and his successor, John Bascom, whose *Aesthetics* was contemporary with the battle of Antietam, write in the same spirit; for the former, "Art, in itself considered, is neither moral nor immoral; it belongs to an entirely separate class of things," while the latter insists that the processes of reasoning and judgment "have no power over Beauty," which is arrived at by the faculty of "internal intuition." Whether these ideas are false or true, one thing is clear: they are thoroughly American, and even though momentarily forgotten, are an integral part of the heritage of American criticism.

If we have forgotten these utterances, it is because they have remained more or less isolated, and their implications but half apprehended; they have never been consolidated into a body of thought or imposed themselves as a state of mind on American critics. For virtually all of us every critical problem is a separate problem, a problem in a philosophic vacuum, and so open for discussion to any astute mind with a taste for letters. Realism, classicism, romanticism, imagism, impressionism, expressionism, and other terms or movements as they spring up, seem ultimate realities instead of matters of very subordinate concern to any philosophy of art,—mere practical programmes which bear somewhat the same relation to aesthetic truth that the platform of the Republican Party bears to Aristotle's *Politics* or Marx's *Capital*.

As a result, critics are constantly carrying on a guerilla warfare of their own in favour of some vague literary shibboleth or sociological abstraction, and discovering anew the virtues or vices of individuality, modernity, Puritanism, the romantic spirit or the spirit of the Middle West, the traditions of the pioneer, and so on ad infinitum. This holds true of every school of American criticism, "conservative" or "radical"; for nearly all of them a disconnected body of literary theories takes the place of a real philosophy of art. "Find an idea and then write about it" sums up the average American writer's conception of criticism. There are even those who conceive this scattering of casual thoughts as the sole duty of a critic, on the extraordinary assumption that in this dispersion of thought and power the critic is "expressing himself" as an "artist." Now, while the critic must approach a work of literature without preconceived notion of what that individual work should attempt, he cannot criticise it without some understanding of what all literature attempts. The critic without an aesthetic is a mariner without chart, compass, or knowledge of navigation; for the question is not where the ship should go or what cargo it should carry, but whether it is going to arrive at any port at all without sinking.

Criticism is essentially an expression of taste, or that faculty of imaginative sympathy by which the reader or spectator is able to relive the vision created by the artist. This is the soil without which it cannot flourish; but it attains its end and becomes criticism in the highest sense only when taste is guided by knowledge and rises to the level of thought, for then, and only then, does the critic give us something that the artist as artist cannot give. Of these three elements, implicit in all real criticism, the professors have made light of taste, and have made thought itself subservient to knowledge, while the dilettanti have considered it possible to dispense with both knowledge and thought. But even dilettante criticism is preferable to the dogmatic and intellectualist criticism of the professors, on the same grounds that Sainte-Beuve is

superior to Brunetière, or Hazlitt to Francis Jef-
frey; for the dilettante at least meets the mind of
the artist on the plane of imagination and taste,
while the intellectualist or moralist is precluded
by his temperament and his theories from ever understanding the primal thrill and purpose of the
creative act.

Back of any philosophy of art there must be a
philosophy of life, and all aesthetic formulae seem
empty unless there is richness of content behind
them. To define criticism without defining art, to
define art without distinguishing it from philosophy and history, and to make this distinction without some understanding of the meaning of philosophy and history themselves, can only be compared with the mythical tasks of Tantalus. So that
the critic, like the poet or the philosopher, has the
whole world to range in, and the farther he
ranges in it, the better his work will be. Yet this
does not mean that criticism, in so far as it remains
criticism of the arts of expression, should focus
its attention on morals, history, life, instead of on
the forms into which the artist transforms them.
Art has something else to give us; and to seek

moral or economic theories in it is to seek moral or economic theories, but not art. It is true that art is the product of human personality, and that personality has little meaning when divorced from moral personality, that is, from some actual or imaginative sense of moral values; but out of that moral personality must be created an aqueduct or an airplane, a treatise on logic or chemistry, a poem or a picture, and a host of other products whose excellence must be judged by their own standards, without reference to ethics. The personality behind the poem or the picture is merely, as it were, inchoate material and not the new and essential *form* that distinguishes the work of art. Even in the larger sense in which a poem may be said to be moral in so far as it aims at unity and order, at some relation with the whole of life, we may ask whether the aesthetic order is identical with the moral order, or whether we have not here two commensurate but not identical planes or aspects of life.

But "to those who cannot understand the voice of Nature or Poetry, unless it speak in apothegms, and tag each story with a moral," as

Margaret Fuller put it nearly eighty years ago, "I have nothing to say." A critic guilty of the incredible assertion that Goethe almost failed of being a great poet merely because he makes Mephistopheles say, "I am the spirit that denies," may be a distinguished moralist, but has completely failed to apprehend the meaning both of criticism and of poetry. The United States is the only civilised country where moral judgment takes precedence over aesthetic judgment when face to face with a work of art; France, Germany, and Italy liberated themselves from this faded obsession long ago, except for a few unimportant reactionary cliques; even in England critics of authority hesitate to make moral standards the first and foremost tests of critical judgment. Yet this is precisely what divides the two chief schools of American criticism, the moralists and the anti-moralists, though even among the latter masquerade some whose only quarrel with the moralists is the nature of the moral standards employed. The seeds of a more fruitful tradition had been planted in our earlier criticism, as we have seen, but the seed had been left to wither and bore no ample fruit.

The main forces that have influenced the present clashes in the American attitude toward literature seem to be three. There is first of all the conception of literature as a moral influence, a conception which goes back to the Graeco-Roman rhetoricians and moralists, and after pervading English thought from Sidney to Johnson, finds its last stronghold today among the American descendants of the Puritans. There is, secondly, the Shavian conception of literature as the most effective instrument for the conversion of the world to a new *Weltanschauung*, to be judged by the novelty and freshness of its ideas, a conception particularly attractive to the school of young reformers, radicals, and intellectuals whose interest in the creative imagination is secondary, and whose training in aesthetic thought has been negligible; this is merely an obverse of the Puritan moralism, and is tainted by the same fundamental misconception of the meaning of the creative imagination. And there is finally the conception of literature as an external thing, a complex of rhythms, charm, technical skill, beauty without inner content, or mere theatrical effectiveness, which goes back through the English 'nineties to the French 'seventies, when the idea of the spiritual autonomy of art,—that "beauty is its own excuse for being,"— was distorted into the merely mechanical theory of "art for art's sake"; the French have a special talent for narrowing aesthetic truths into hard-and-fast formulae, devoid of their original nucleus of philosophic reality, but all the more effective on this account for universal conquest as practical programmes.

All three of these conceptions have their element of truth, but all three are inadequate and incomplete. Works of literature, as mere documents, provide important material for history; the winged words of great poets have had a profound moral and social influence; the prophetic quality of the imagination gives its message an explosive force; and the technique of art is part of the material out of which the artist fashions his creations. All this the historian of culture may, indeed must, take into consideration; out of these elements the moralist or the aesthete may draw material for his studies; yet to rest the case here is to ignore the essential problem of art. Pity the poor aesthete, for whom art, in any of its single outer manifestations, is the whole life of the spirit; pity the poor moralist for whom the life of the spirit in one of its highest moments is cribbed and confined by a narrow theory of the meaning of art and life. It may be difficult to tell which of them misses the most; yet who can doubt that when we meet them in practical life the error of the moralist seems the nobler of the two? And how could it be otherwise?—for it is precisely in the life of action that we seek for the guiding star of moral values, which the aesthete attempts to evade in assuming that the ideal freedom of the artist as an artist is one with the practical duty of the artist as a man. But in the ideal world of art moralism must always find itself homeless and dispossessed. The very nature of poetry must forever be a bitter challenge to those who have only this narrow single standard; and there is no other way out except that of Plato, who because of the "immorality" of poetry banishes all poets forever from the ideal Republic. Of all the moralistic critics, Plato is one of the very few who are thoroughly consistent.

The American Critic

The apparent paradox which none of these critics face is that the *Weltanschauung* of the creative artist, his moral convictions, his views on intellectual, economic, and other subjects, furnish the content of his work and are at the same time the chief obstacles to his artistic achievement. Out of morals or philosophy he has to make, not morals or philosophy, but poetry; for morals and philosophy are only a part, and a small part, of the whole reality which his imagination has to encompass. The man who is overwhelmed with moral theories and convictions would naturally find it easiest to become a moralist, and moralists are prosaic, not poetic. A man who has strong economic convictions would find it easiest to become an economist or economic reformer, and economic theory as well as practice is also the prose of life, not the poetry. A man with a strong philosophic bias would find it easiest to become a pure thinker, and the poet's visionary world topples when laid open to the cold scrutiny of logic. A poet is a human being, and therefore likely to have convictions, prejudices, preconceptions, like other men; but the deeper his interest in them is, the easier it is for him to become a moralist, economist, philosopher, or what not, and the harder (without the divine aid of the Muses) to transcend them and to become a poet.

But if the genius of the poet (and by poet I mean any writer of imaginative literature) is strong enough, it will transcend them, pass over them by the power of the imagination, which leaves them behind without knowing it. It has been well said that morals are one reality, a poem is another reality, and the illusion consists in thinking them one and the same. The poet's conscience as a man may be satisfied by the illusion, but woe to him if it is not an illusion, for that is what we tell him when we say, "He is a moralist, not a poet." Such a man has merely expressed his moral convictions, instead of *leaping over and beyond them* into that world of the imagination where moral ideas must be interpreted from the standpoint of poetry, or the artistic needs of the characters portrayed, and not by the logical or reality value of morals. When we say with Emerson that beauty, like truth, is "an ultimate end," the narrow moralist or the man of practical mind assumes that we are giving advice to the dilettante trifler in verse (who is not an artist at all) instead of attempting to define the essential secret of the art of Aeschylus and Dante, Shakespeare and Goethe, Milton and Racine, and all their high compeers, classic and romantic, in the ancient and modern world. But how can we solve that secret if we see no difference whatever between their art and the thought of a Plato or Spinoza, the moral illumination of an Emerson or Franklin, or the noble exaltation of the Gettysburg Address? The critic who has missed that difference has missed everything. By ignoring one of the vital elements necessary to form a synthesis, he has even missed the power of understanding their essential unity in the life of the spirit.

That is what we mean when we say that this "leaping over" is the test of all art, that it is inherent in the very nature of the creative imagination. It explains a myriad problems. It explains, for example, how Milton the moralist started out to make Satan a demon and how Milton the poet ended by making him a hero; and from this "hymning of the devil" we learn how our moralistic critics cannot understand even a Puritan poet. From another angle, it explains the blindness of the American critic who recently objected to the "loose thinking" of Carl Sandburg's poem, *Smoke and Steel*, in which steel is conceived as made of "smoke and blood," and who propounded this question to the Walrus and the Carpenter: "How can smoke, the lighter refuse of steel, be one of its constituents, and how can the smoke which drifts away from the chimney and the blood which flows in the steelmaker's veins be correlates in their relation to steel?"

Where shall we match this precious gem? Over two centuries ago, Othello's cry after the death of Desdemona,

> "O heavy hour,
> Methinks it should now be a huge eclipse
> Of sun and moon!"

provoked another intellectualistic critic to inquire whether "the sun and moon can both together be so hugely eclipsed in any one heavy hour whatsoever"; but Rymer has been called "the worst critic that ever lived" for applying tests like these to the poetry of Shakespeare. Over a century ago a certain Abbé Morellet, unmoved by the music of Chateaubriand's description of the moon,—

"She pours forth in the woods this great secret of melancholy which she loves to recount to the old oaks and the ancient shores of the sea,"—

asked his readers: "How can the melancholy of night be called a secret; and if the moon recounts it, how is it still a secret; and how does she manage to recount it to the old oaks and the ancient shores of the sea rather than to the deep valleys, the mountains, and the rivers?" And so when Macbeth, stung by his agony into immortal eloquence, —"tomorrow and tomorrow and tomorrow,"— finds time but a petty pace that has lighted fools the way to dusty death, and life itself nothing but a tale

"Told by an idiot, full of sound and fury,
Signifying nothing,"

can we not imagine some of our own professors, for whom Art is but a pretty page serving King Virtue and Queen Truth, crying out in disdain: "And it is this passage, gentlemen, in which a false and im-

moral conception of life is expounded, that some
of the so-called aesthetic critics consider the high-
water mark of poetry"? Or if we cannot imagine it,
it is only because the passage is not by a modern
poet without the prestige of Shakespeare's fame.

These are simply exaggerations of the inevitable
consequence of subjecting the world of the imagination to the moods and tests of actual life. "Sense,
sense, nothing but sense!" cried a great Austrian
poet, "as if poetry in contrast with prose were not
always a kind of divine nonsense. Every poetic
image bears within itself its own certain demon-
stration that logic is not the arbitress of art." And
Alfieri spoke for every poet in the world when he
said of himself, "Reasoning and judging are for
me only pure and generous forms of feeling."
The trained economist, philosopher, or moralist,
examining the ideas of a poet, is always likely to
say: "These are not clearly thought out or logical
ideas; they are just a poet's fancy or inspiration";
and the sneer of the expert may be the final praise
of the poet. To give us a vision of reality, and
not reality, imagination rather than thought or
morals, is the eternal mission of the artist. To

forego that vision is to miss one of the highest moments of the life of the spirit. No other experience can serve as a substitute; no life that has not known it can regard itself as completely fulfilled.

These are some of the elementary reasons why those who demand of the poet a definite code of morals or manners, the ready-made standards of any society, however great, that is bounded by space or time—"American ideals," or "Puritanism," or on the other side, "radical ideas"—seem to me to show their incompetence as critics. Life, teeming life, with all its ardors and agonies, is the only limit within which the poet's vision can be cabined and confined; and all we ask of him is that he create a new life in which the imagination can breathe and move as naturally as our practical selves can live in the world of reality. How can we expect illumination from critics who share the "typical American business man's" inherent inability to live in the world of fantasy which the poets have created, without the business man's ability to face the external facts of life and mould them to his will? These men are schoolmasters, pedants, moralists, policemen, but neither critics nor true lovers of the spiritual food that art provides. To the creative writers of America I should give a wholly different message from theirs. I should say to them: "Express what is in you, all that serene or turbulent vision of multitudinous life which is yours by right of imagination, trusting in your own power to achieve discipline and mastery, and leave the theoretical discussion of 'American ideals' to statesmen, historians, and philosophers, with the certainty that if you truly express the vision of your highest self, the statesmen, historians, and philosophers of the future will point to your work as a fine expression of the 'American ideals' you have helped to create. Do not wait for the flux of time to create a society that you can copy, but create your own society; and if you are a great writer it will be a Great Society, which the world will never cease to live in and to love. For you America must always be not old but new, something unrealised, something to be created and to be given as an incredible gift to a hundred million men. Courage is the birthright of the poet as much as of the soldier or statesman; and courage in trusting your imagination is to you the very breath of life. But mastery of the imagination, and not mere submission to it, must be your goal; for how can the true artist express himself in terms of slavery rather than power? By giving what is best in him to his art, the American artist serves America best."

A profound inner reform is needed in order that the critics of America may prepare themselves adequately to interpret this new literature, to separate the chaff from the wheat, and in so doing to purify and ennoble the taste and enlarge the imaginative sympathies of a whole people.

The first need of American criticism today is education in aesthetic thinking. It needs above all the cleansing and stimulating power of an intellectual bath. Only the drenching discipline that comes from mastery of the problems of aesthetic thought can train us for the duty of interpreting the American literature of the future. The anarchy of impressionism is a natural reaction against the mechanical theories and jejune text-books of the professors, but it is a temporary haven and not a home. The haphazard empiricism of English criticism and the faded moralism of some of our own will serve us no more. We must desert these muddy waters, and seek purer and deeper streams. For the conception of the critic as censor or as eulogist we must substitute the conception of the critic as aesthetic thinker. In a country where philosophers urge men to cease thinking, it may be the task of the critic to revivify and reorganise thought.

The second need of American criticism can be summed up in the word scholarship—that discipline of knowledge which will give us at one and the same time a wider international outlook and a deeper national insight. One will spring from the other, for the timid colonial spirit finds no place in the heart of the citizen of the world; and respect for native talent, born of a surer knowledge, will prevent us alike from overrating its merits and from holding it too cheap. For the lifeless pedantry of the antiquarians, who think that tradition actually lives in monuments, heirlooms, dead ancestors, and printed books, we must substitute the illumination of a humane scholarship, which realises that learning is but a quest for the larger

self and that tradition is a state of the soul. Half-
knowledge is either too timid or too cocksure; and
only out of the spiritual discipline that is born of
intellectual travail and adventure can come a true
independence of judgment and taste.

For taste is after all both the point of departure
and the goal; and the third and at this moment the
greatest need of American criticism is a deeper
sensibility, a more complete submission to the
imaginative will of the artist, before attempting
to rise above it into the realm of judgment. The
critic is not a man seated on a block of ice watching
a bright fire, or how could he realise the full force
of its warmth and power? If there is anything that
American life can be said to give least of all, it is
training in taste. There is a deadness of artistic
feeling, which is sometimes replaced or disguised
by a fervor of sociological obsession, but this is
no substitute for the faculty of imaginative sympathy which is at the heart of all criticism. By
taste, I mean, of course, not the "good taste" of
the dilettante or the amateur collector, or taste in
its eighteenth-century sense, but that creative moment of the life of the spirit which the artist and

the enjoyer of art share alike. For this the ardour of the reformer, the insight of the historian, even the moral passion of the saint is no substitute; for taste, or disciplined aesthetic enjoyment, is the only gateway to the critic's judgment, and over it is a flaming signpost, "Critic, abandon all hope when this gate is shut."

This is your task, critics of America—to see that Plato's dream of banishing poets from the ideal Republic does not come true. It is your chief duty, against moralist and hedonist and utilitarian alike, to justify the ways of the artist to Americans. In a land where virtuous platitudes have so often been mistaken for poetry, it is your task to explain the real meaning of the aesthetic moment for the higher lives of men. But no one knows better than I that you cannot rest satisfied even with this. For the modern critic has learnt to distinguish clearly between art, philosophy, history, religion, morals, not for the purpose of denying but of establishing their essential unity in the life of the spirit. Those who deny this unity and those who would substitute for it a muddle-headed if well-meaning confusion are alike the Enemy. Though you reject the criticism in which art is forever measured and tested by the moralist's rigid rules and justified by virtues that are not her own, still less can you be satisfied with the criticism in which "ideas" are struck out in random and irresponsible flashes like sparks from the anvil of a gnome. You cannot be satisfied with anything but truth—that whole truth which is life—even in the service of art and beauty.

The American Scholar

A LAMENT

IT IS natural for the musician to think any land
barbarous if it has produced no great com-
posers, the painter if it has produced no great
painters, the critic or the scholar if it has produced
no great scholars and critics, and so on for all the
other arts and sciences. But it is idle to insist that
every race should express itself in the same way,
or to assume that the genius of a nation can be
tested by its deficiencies in any single field of the
higher life. Great critics are rare in every age and
country; and even if they were not, what consola-
tion is there for the clash and diversity of races
and nations except the special and diverse gifts
which each may furnish to the spiritual whole?
England has achieved greatness without great
music, Germany without great sculpture, ancient
Rome without great science or philosophy, Judaea
with little but poetry and religion; and it is not

necessary to lay too much stress on our own lack
of great scholars and great critics—yes, even on
our lack of great poets and great painters. They
may come today or tomorrow, or we may be destined never to have them. The idea that great
national energy must inevitably flower in a great
literature, and that our wide-flung power must certainly find expression in an immortal poem or in
the "great American novel," is merely another example of our mechanical optimism. The vision of
great empires that have left no enduring literature, Assyria, Babylonia, Egypt, haunts all history; even Virgil or Camoens only fitfully expresses the power that is summed up in Caesar or
Magellan.

But without insisting on impossible aims or
illusory standards of greatness, it is fair to ask
some flow of spiritual activity, some general spirit
of diffused culture. For though we must eat (and
common sense will cook better dinners than philosophy), though we must work (and the captain
of industry can organise trade better than the
poet), though we must play (and the athlete can
win more games than the scholar), the civilisation

that has no higher outlets for its intellect and imagination will show at least some marks of spiritual starvation. You may see the signs of its restless gnawing on the faces of far too many American women beyond the first flush of youth; you may see some shadow of its hopeless craving on the faces of far too many American men.

The same signs are to be seen in American scholarship and American criticism. If scholarship were what most people think it, the dull learning of pedants, and criticism merely the carping and bickering of fault-finders, the fact would hardly be worth recording. But since they are instruments which the mind of man uses for some of its keenest questionings, their absence or their weakness must indicate something at least in the national life and character which it is not unimportant to understand.

The tradition of scholarship, like so many other things, comes to us from what used to be called the Renaissance, the period (it may not be ironical to be reminded) in which the Americas were discovered and explored; and whatever savour of distinction inheres in the idea of "the gentleman and the scholar" was created then. Scholarship at first meant merely a knowledge of the classics, and though it has since widened its scope, even then the diversity of its problems was apparent, for the classical writers had tilled many fields of human knowledge, and the student of Homer and Virgil was really faced with a different problem from the student of Plato or Thucydides. Scholarship has never been a reality, a field that could be bounded and defined in the sense in which poetry, philosophy, and history can be. It is a point of view, an attitude, a method of approach, and, so far as its meaning and purpose can be captured, it may be said to be the discipline and illumination that come from the intellectual mastery of a definite problem involved in the growth of the human spirit.

Scholarship, conceived in this sense, has no history (though dull and learned hodge-podges have served as such), for it is a spirit diffused over various fields of study; and in America this spirit has been isolated and sporadic, rather than general and diffused. American Universities seem to have been created for the special purpose of ignoring or destroying it. The chief monuments of American scholarship have seldom if ever come from men who have been willing to live their whole lives in an academic atmosphere. The men whom we think of as our foremost literary scholars, Gildersleeve, Norton, and the rest, acquired their fame rather through their personalities than their scholarly achievements. The historians, Motley, Prescott, Bancroft, Parkman, Rhodes, Lea, Fiske, Mahan, were not professors; books like Taylor's *Mediaeval Mind*, Henry Adams's *Mont Saint Michel and Chartres*, Thayer's *Cavour*, Villard's *John Brown*, and Beveridge's *John Marshall*, even Ticknor's *History of Spanish Literature*, were not written within University walls, though Ticknor's sixteen years of teaching tamed the work of a brilliant man of the world until there is little left save the characteristic juiceless virtue of an intelligent ordering of laborious research. It would seem as if in the atmosphere of our Universities personality could not find fruitage in scholarly achievement worthy of it, and learning can only thrive when it gives no hostages to the enemy, personality.

The American Scholar

Of the typical products of this academic system, the lowest is perhaps the literary dissertation and the highest the historical manual or text-book. It may be because history is not my own special field of study that I seem to find its practitioners more vigorous intellectually than the literary scholars. Certainly the distinguished work of Breasted, Haskins, and others deserves a passing tribute. But for the most part our historians seem to have a special aptitude for compiling careful summaries of historical periods, and some of these have an ordered reasonableness and impersonal efficiency not unlike that of the financial accounting system of our large trusts or the budgets of our large universities. To me most of them seem feats of historical engineering rather than of historical scholarship; and if they represent a scholarly "advance" on older and less accurate work, written before Clio became a peon of the professors, it can only be said that history has not yet recovered from the advance. Nor am I as much impressed as the historians themselves by the more recent clash between the "old" school and the "new," for both seem to me equally lacking in a truly philosophic conception of the meaning of history. In fact, the "new history," in its childish subservience to the empirical sciences, and the shallow and extrinsic character of its thought, has lost sight of the very essence of the nature of history. But among the younger breed in general there is a certain freshness of mind and an openness to new ideas, though less to the problems of human personality or to the emotional and spiritual values of man's life. All are still immersed in the search for external causes, and fail to realise that the idea of causality in history belongs to the past and not to the future.

But literary scholarship is in far worse plight in our Universities. Few if any great works on classical literature have ever been achieved by American scholars. It may be unfair to suggest comparison with men like Gilbert Murray, Croiset, or Wilamowitz, not to mention Scaliger or Casaubon; but how can we be persuaded by the professors or even by a dean that all culture will die if we forget Greek and Latin, until they satisfy us by their own work that they themselves are alive? Asia beckons to us with the hand of Fate, but Oriental literary scholarship is a desert through which

a few nomadic professors wander aimlessly. As
to the literatures in the modern European tongues,
Dante scholarship has perhaps the oldest and
most respectable tradition, but on examination
dwindles into its proper proportions: an essay by
Lowell and translations by Longfellow and Norton pointed the way; a Dante Society has nursed
it; and its modern fruits, with a few honourable
exceptions, are for the most part unilluminating
articles and text-books. Ticknor's pioneer work in
the Spanish field has had no successors, though
Spanish America is at our doors; the generous sub-
sidies of rich men have resulted as usual in build-
ings but not in scholarship. Of the general level
of our French and German studies I prefer to say
nothing; and silence is also wisest in the case of
English. This field fairly teems with professors;
Harvard has twice as many as Oxford and Cam-
bridge combined, and the University of Chicago
almost as many as the whole of England. Whether
this plethora of professors has justified itself,
either by distinguished works of scholarship or by
helping young America to love literature and to
write good English, I shall not decide, but leave

entirely to their own conscience. This at least may be said, that the mole is not allowed to burrow in his hole without disturbance; for in this atmosphere, as a protest and counterfoil, or as a token of submission to the idols of the marketplace, there has arisen a very characteristic academic product, —the professor who writes popular articles, sometimes clever, sometimes precious, sometimes genteel and refined, sometimes merely commonplace, but almost always devoid of real knowledge or stimulating thought. Even the sober pedant is a more humane creature than the professorial smart-Aleck.

Whence arises this academic inhibition of mediocrity, this fear of personality and intellect, this deep antinomy of pedant and dilettante? If I were a sociologist, confident that the proper search would unearth an external cause for every spiritual defect, I might point to any one of a dozen or more damning facts as the origin and source of all our trouble,—to the materialism of a national life directed solely toward practical ends, to the levelling and standardising influences of democracy, to Anglo-Saxon "colonialism," to the influence of German erudition, or to the inadequate economic rewards of the academic life. I should probably make much of that favourite theme of critical fantasy, the habits derived from the "age of the pioneers," a period in which life, with its mere physical discomforts and its mere demands on physical energy and endurance, was really so easy and simple that Americans attempt to reproduce it on all their holidays. But all these are merely symptoms of the same disease of the soul. They are facts and not determining factors of history, which knows no external causes, but only the great generating forces, religious and ethical, which move men to transform circumstance into a new life. A religion that has built skyscrapers and factories and conquered a continent is inadequate to give central meaning to institutions of higher learning. We have not yet created anew "The Idea of a University." The mere cult of accuracy is no substitute for a faith, a religion, a profoundly felt philosophy of life.

The modern sanatorium may be likened to a mediaeval monastery which has substituted practical skill for spiritual faith. The American University is in this sense modern too: it is an intellectual refuge in which practical skill has taken the place of inner illumination and integration,— crassly material because it has no inner standards to redeem it from the idols of the marketplace, or timid and anaemic because it lacks that quixotic fire which inheres in every act of faith. It is at one and the same time our greatest practical achievement and our greatest spiritual failure. When we find that in such a place education does not educate, we cry for help to the only gods we know, the restless gods of Administration and Organisation; but scholarship cannot be organised or administered into existence, even by Americans. The scholar goes through all the proper motions,— collects facts, organises research, delivers lectures, writes articles and sometimes books,—but under this outer seeming there is no inner reality. Under all the great works of culture there broods the quivering soul of tradition, a burden sometimes disturbing and heavy to bear, but more often helping the soul to soar on wings not of its own making. We think hungrily that the freshness of outlook of a young people should be more than compensation; but the freshness is not there. All is shell, mask, and a deep inner emptiness. We have scholars without scholarship, as there are churches without religion.

Until there comes a change of heart or a new faith or a deep inner searching, scholarship must continue to live this thwarted and frustrated life. Only a profound realisation of its high purpose and special function, and the pride that comes from this realisation, can give the scholar his true place in an American world. For this special function is none other than to act as the devoted servant of thought and imagination and to champion their claims as the twin pillars that support all the spiritual activities of human life,—poetry, art, philosophy, religion, history; and these it must champion against all the materialists under whatever name they disguise their purpose. What matter whether they be scientists who decry "dialectics," or sociologists who sneer at "mere literature," or practical men who have no use for the "higher life"? Whether they be called bourgeois or radical, conservative or intellectual,—all who would reduce life to a problem of practical activity and physical satisfaction, all who would reduce intellect and imagination to mere instruments of practical usefulness, all who worship dead idols instead of living gods, all who grasp at every flitting will-o'-the-wisp of theory or sensation,—all these alike scholarship must forever recognise as its enemies and its chief tempters.

We are all cocksure but bewildered children in a world we cannot understand. We are all newcomers—newcomers on a new continent, on the fringes of which some have. lived longer than others, but the *whole* of which has been encompassed by none of us for more than two or three generations; newcomers in a world of steam and electricity, wireless and aeroplane, machinery and industry, which none of us has yet been able to subdue to a mould that satisfies our deepest cravings; newcomers in our culture, which still seems like a borrowed garment instead of flesh of our flesh and bone of our bone. What is the good of all the instruments that our hands have moulded if we have neither the will nor the imagination to wield them for the uses of the soul? Not in this fashion shall we justify our old dream of an America that is the hope of the world. Here are hundreds of colleges and universities; why not fill these crowded yet empty barracks with scholars and thinkers? Here are a hundred races; why not say to them: "America can give you generous opportunity and the most superb instruments that the undisciplined energy of practical life has ever created, but in the spiritual fields of art, poetry, religion, culture, though it has noble elements in its brief tradition, it has still much to learn and to create; let us all work together, learning and creating these high things side by side"? Here are more hearts empty and unfulfilled and more restless minds than the world has ever before gathered together; why not lead them out of their corrals, and find a fitting pasture for their brains and souls?

The Growth of a Literary Myth

MR. H. L. MENCKEN, the enemy of all my-
thologies and religions, is himself the creator of a literary myth. In the first series of his
Prejudices it sprang full-grown into life. There
he created the four-headed monster which he
christened the "Croce-Spingarn-Carlyle-Goethe
theory," and which was intended to serve as the
titular deity for all the ideas found in a volume
of essays entitled *Creative Criticism*. The monster
has developed a vigour that threatens to make
light of infant mortality; it has even developed
the power of the amoeba to split up into parts each
with a life of its own. So Mr. George Jean Nathan,
in his recent book on *The Critic and the Theatre*,
takes as the starting point of his whole discussion
something that he calls "the Goethe-Carlyle
theory," which seems to be a theory of dramatic
criticism in some way related to Mr. Mencken's
more inclusive "Croce-Spingarn-Goethe-Carlyle
theory" of criticism in general. So, too, Mr. Pierre

A Literary Myth

Loving, in a still more recent review of *The Drama in Transition*, tells us that "the Croce-Spingarn theory (a patent offshoot of that espoused by Goethe and Carlyle) categorically secludes drama in a place apart from the theatre." If I were not writing in a place that is rich in climate but poor in books, I should have no difficulty in adding several other illustrations of the vitality with which Mr. Mencken's creation lives.

Alas, there is no "Croce-Spingarn-Goethe-Carlyle theory," or if there is, then only in a very restricted sense. Certainly there is no "Goethe-Carlyle theory of the drama" such as Mr. Nathan and Mr. Loving and the rest imagine. If there is a "Croce-Spingarn theory" (of the drama or anything else) it owes no direct debt to Goethe or Carlyle. Indeed, it is a question whether it is fair to one far greater than I to call the theory of dramatic criticism which I have developed "the Croce-Spingarn theory," for Mr. A. B. Walkley once filled two columns of the London *Times* with proofs that my theory is not good Crocean doctrine, and perhaps he is right.

The confusion, I imagine, came about somewhat

in this way. Years ago, at the very outset of the so-called "American Renaissance," I attempted, among other things, to make some of the implications of Croce's aesthetic theory clear to Americans. I was not expounding Croce (I have left that to others); I was making use of him for the benefit of my countrymen. Croce was writing in a country whose chief living men of letters were Carducci and D'Annunzio. I was writing for an audience that read with respect if not with pleasure the work of Hamilton Wright Mabie and Richard Watson Gilder. I did not hesitate therefore to make my own use of the material Croce afforded me; and the result, for better or for worse, is a very one-sided introduction to Croce's thought, and is responsible, I fear, for some of the misapprehensions in regard to his ideas that exist in America today. How many a phrase have I seen quoted as Croce which happened to be only Spingarn—or perhaps even Spingarn's misstatement of Croce. Many years ago, in the days of my scholarly apprenticeship, I pointed out that Sir Philip Sidney's *Defence of Poesie* was in no sense original, but was largely borrowed from the Italian critics Scaliger and Minturno, and that Ben Jonson's *Timber, or Discoveries* was hardly more than a cento of translations from the Dutch and other critics of his time, just as Horace's *Ars Poetica* was largely borrowed from the Greek of Neoptolemus of Parium, or Du Bellay's famous manifesto in defence of the French language from the Italian of Sperone Speroni, or much of Coleridge's criticism from the German of Schlegel; and though these borrowings detracted not a whit from their actual achievements, I learnt from this study of my betters how unfair it is to hold the originals responsible for the utterances of their disciples and debtors, when even a change of tone or rhythm of speech may twist or pervert, or give a new individuality to, the original thought. But my sin would be great indeed if I were in any way responsible for the fact that Croce, a master of logical distinctions, has been regarded by some Americans as the advocate or abettor of "emotional debauch" in aesthetic theory or critical practice—Croce, who in Italy has come to be regarded more and more as the leader of a classical reaction intended to transcend romanticism without losing sight of its permanent values, and who has been called by the more morbidly romantic of his countrymen "intellectualistic," "moralistic," and even "prosaic."

Now, it so happened that while I was writing one of my essays I came upon two passages in Goethe and Carlyle which seemed to reinforce Croce's conception of criticism, and so I quoted them. They were the passages in which it is said that the critic should concern himself with the poet's own intentions and not with rules laid down by others; that the critic should especially ask of any creative work: "What has the writer proposed to himself to do, and how well has he succeeded in carrying out his own plan?" It is one of Goethe's most casual utterances, let slip in one of his essays and never elaborated; it is repeated by Carlyle in his essay on Goethe; and, long forgotten, it has now apparently become the rallying cry of quite a number of our younger critics. Understood rightly, it does explain exactly what I intended it should; understood literally, as it seems to have been misunderstood by virtually the whole of that tiny minority which reads what I write, it completely distorts not only Croce's meaning but any possible truth. For the "intentions" of a writer, in the literal sense of that word, may be of no more concern to his critics than the colour of his hair. Literature, like hell, is paved with good intentions; Milton's nephew, Edward Phillips, said truly that every poet *intends* to write a good poem. Milton himself intended to write a classical epic, and Addison judged him largely by his success in carrying out this intention; but in so doing, Addison sinned against the central spirit of modern criticism, which has found another method of judging artistic excellence than agreement or disagreement with external and mechanical standards.

The poet's real "intention" is to be found, not in one or another of the various ambitions that flit through his mind, but in the actual work of art which he creates. His poem is his "intention." In any other sense, "intention" is outside the aesthetic field—a mere matter of the poet's literary theory or his power of will—and so matter for the biographer of the man rather than for the critic of the poem. Croce himself quotes as an early antici-

pation of his thought on this point a couplet from
Pope's *Essay on Criticism:*

> "A perfect judge will read each work of wit
> With the same spirit that its author writ."

This is closer to the truth, and less liable to mis-
apprehension, than the passages from Goethe and
Carlyle; for it is the creative "spirit" and not mere
volition or "intention" that is concerned—the spirit
in which the author actually writes and not what
he intended to write. When I had occasion to reprint the essay in which the Goethe-Carlyle passages were first quoted, I added a *caveat* against
this possible misinterpretation, to the effect that
the "intention" of the author must be sought in
the work of art itself. But even this was not suf-
ficient, for Mr. Burton Rascoe has recently asserted that the idea of "intention" is the basis of
the whole Crocean system, and has challenged me
to tell what Shakespeare "intended" at the moment when he sat down to write *The Phoenix and
the Turtle.* Yet whatever may have been Shakespeare's "intention" in Mr. Rascoe's sense (not
mine), no criticism of that poem or any other poem

is possible without a realisation of "the spirit in which its author writ." To say that a work of art is achieved when the expression, the artistic intuition, is complete, that is, when the crude material in the mind of the artist has been given artistic form, is quite a different thing from saying that it has been achieved when the artist by an act of mere volition has carried out a prearranged plan. Certainly nothing could be more wholly un-Crocean than to judge an artist by his intentions, in the literal sense, as distinguished from his achievements.

In other words, the idea of "intention" was introduced merely to reinforce the central thought of "The New Criticism," a thought for which there is also confirmation in a casual utterance of Goethe: "If you read a book and let it work upon you, and yield yourself up entirely to its influence, then, and only then, will you arrive at a correct judgment of it." But yielding to the "influence" of a book is only the preparatory, though an essential and indispensable, duty of the critic; and Goethe's thought is nowhere more completely expressed than in Carlyle's *Essay on Goethe:* "First, we must have made plain to ourselves what the poet's aim really and truly was, how the task he had to do stood before his own eye, and how far, with such means as it afforded him, he has fulfilled it. Secondly, we must have decided whether and how far this aim, this task of his, accorded,—not with *us*, and our individual crotchets, and the crotchets of our little senate where we give or take the law,—but with human nature, and the nature of things at large; with the universal principles of poetic beauty, not as they stand written in our text-books, but in the hearts and imaginations of all men." I have never doubted the legitimacy of the second of these demands; and if I emphasised the first in the essays of *Creative Criticism* it was because, as I have said, the academic dry rot of that day seemed to need most of all the lesson that the critic must immerse himself in the creative spirit of the artist before he can rise above it to the level of judgment. I have never doubted that art aims at some kind of universality, and that the artist aims at expressing this higher and universal side of himself. Nothing could be clearer than my statement that "the imagination is governed by an inner logic of its own, and not by unreasonable caprice," and if the less intelligent of my critics have assumed that by expression, or self-expression, I have meant the very things that I specifically excluded from it, whim, eccentricity, the habits and manners of the poet's practical personality, I shall on my part charitably assume that this has been due to the ambiguity of the term, "self-expression," which, so far as I remember, Croce himself never employs. Perhaps it would be impossible to make clear to such critics the abyss that separates the naturalistic "expression of the emotions"—as used by the psychologists and by Darwin, or by the so-called "expressionistic" poets and painters—from "expression" in the aesthetic sense in which I have always employed it. Many years ago, in my first book, I committed myself to the statement that "it is with what is permanent and universal that the artist is concerned."

Even these digressions should make it self-evident how absurd it is to call the massive system of Croce a "patent offshoot" of the casual utterances of Goethe and Carlyle, and how (*mea culpa*) the mere accident of quotation is responsible for the absurdity. Only when reinterpreted in a modern sense are these casual utterances true; but whatever their truth, they are mere *obiter dicta* embedded in work that does not attempt to elaborate them. There is no important idea in the world for which such informal, and I might add unimportant, anticipations can not be found. It is true that all modern criticism owes much to the Germans of the age from Herder to Hegel; and every critic who calls a poem a work of art or a novelist an artist pays unconscious tribute to the thinkers who first made us understand that all the forms of the creative imagination are contained in the single concept of *Kunst,* or art. But to say that Goethe and Carlyle are the fathers of the Crocean system because it has been possible to find in their work isolated utterances which seem to anticipate one of the minor incidents of his thought, is on a par with Professor Irving Babbitt's contention that the modern theory of the relation between "genius" and "taste" is not modern at all because two characters in one of Smollett's novels used the words "genius" and "taste" and because Schlegel casually correlated the two terms over a century ago.

A Literary Myth

It is always well to bear in mind what Stirling says in his *Secret of Hegel:* "It is a curious thing that, once a doctrine has·become historically established, we are often startled by expressions in the works of previous writers which seem accurately to describe it; yet these previous writers shall have no more insight into the doctrine concerned than any Indian in his woods; and we ourselves should have found something quite else in the expressions, had we read them before the doctrine itself was become historically overt." This discussion of Goethe and Carlyle may seem ridiculous to the student of philosophy, who knows that Croce's masters were Vico, Hegel, and De Sanctis; but the student of philosophy needs Stirling's admonition no less than the literary critic.

This is not a defence of Croce, but a little contribution to the history of contemporary criticism. In a sense we have "passed beyond" Croce, just as we have passed beyond the immortals who preceded him from the days of Plato; and this is as he himself would have it, for no man has denied more completely than he the idea of finality in thought. But no critic who has not "passed through" him is in a position to understand what modern criticism has really achieved. Has Mr. Mencken passed through him? I re-read the essay in which the "Croce-Spingarn-Goethe-Carlyle theory" is expounded, and this at least seems clear: Mr. Mencken realises that he is face to face with novel and important ideas, whereas his academic opponents do not even realise that. Such prestige as the theory has acquired in America is in some measure due to his generous trumpeting. And yet —and yet—I rub my eyes—what has become of the ideas when infused with his vigorous personality? Is the theory merely a defence of impressionism in criticism, instead of an exposure of its limitations and a pointing to something beyond? And can any man who explains poetic inspiration by "the chemical content of the digestive tract" be said to have "passed through" Croce?

So much for Mr. Mencken's "Croce-Spingarn-Goethe-Carlyle theory." I hardly know how to characterise its offshoot, Mr. Nathan's "Goethe-Carlyle theory of the drama." Mr. Nathan has devoted himself (very wisely, I think) to the work of contemporary playwrights and actors, and has not wasted his time, as I have, in the study of the history and philosophy of criticism. His mental process in this case (without the lively language that must run through so acrobatic a brain) seems to have been something like this: "Spingarn has written an essay on dramatic criticism; he is devoted to Croce, so the ideas in the essay probably came from Croce. But Croce's ideas are apparently based on some passages on the purpose of criticism in general which Spingarn in another essay quotes from Goethe and Carlyle. Evidently, then, Goethe and Carlyle had a theory of dramatic criticism substantially like Spingarn's."

If Mr. Nathan is a sportsman and fond of the chase, I suggest that he spend his next holiday hunting for a theory of dramatic criticism in Carlyle. If he has no luck on that expedition, his next may very well be spent in searching Goethe for a theory that "categorically secludes drama in a place apart from the theatre." As a final jaunt I suggest that he make his way through the jungle of Croce's forty or fifty volumes, in quest of any extended discussion of "the theory of the drama." He will find much to interest him on the way, not least of all Croce's early work on *The Theatres of Naples*, which is still the best book on the subject; he will learn that Croce's youthful *Aesthetic* is a very slender basis for any judgment on Croce's contribution to philosophy, ethics, political and economic theory, history, aesthetics, and literary criticism; and he will discover how much not only I but all modern critics owe to Croce's seminal thought. But he will come out of the jungle, I think, without his earlier conviction that the theory of dramatic criticism which he calls the "Goethe-Carlyle theory" is to be found either in Goethe or in Carlyle, or that Croce is to be blamed for all the obvious weaknesses of my own essay on "Dramatic Criticism and the Theatre."

If he is still unwearied after all this exercise, I suggest that he search the shelves of some great library for a book on *Literary Criticism in the Renaissance* (published several years before Croce's *Aesthetic*), that he blow away the dust that has gathered over it, and turn to its discussion of a sixteenth-century Italian, Castelvetro, whose "theory of the theatre" anticipates that of William Archer, Brander Matthews, and Professor Baker.

A Literary Myth

There Mr. Nathan will find my youthful answer to Castelvetro's theory.[1] There he will see how early in life I acquired a distaste for this "theory of the theatre," for the "well-made play," and for all the rest of the shallow doctrine current in our time. There he will find, briefly but explicitly stated, the conception of dramatic criticism which has been mine from the beginning, and which Croce and a host of other critics and thinkers have given me arguments to explain and defend. To describe that conception as "categorically secluding the drama apart from the theatre" is to misunderstand its meaning, for it is concerned with neither drama nor theatre on a merely empirical plane. It is based on the idea—call it faith, if you will—

[1] "But Castelvetro's method brings with it its own reductio ad absurdum. For after all, stage representation, while essential to the production of dramatic literature, can never circumscribe the poetic power or establish its conditions. The conditions of stage representation change, and must change, with the varying conditions of dramatic literature and the inventive faculty of poets, for truly great art makes, or at least fixes, its own conditions. Besides, it is with what is permanent and universal that the artist—the dramatic artist as well as the rest—is concerned; and it is the poetic, and not the dramaturgic, element that is permanent and universal."—*Literary Criticism in the Renaissance*, 1899, page 71.

that the artist is not created by external conditions but in a sense creates them, and that criticism, therefore, whether of the drama or of any other form of the creative imagination, must look to the inner life of art, and not to external conditions or mechanical tests, as the basis for its judgments.

APPENDIX

Non Credo

(LETTER TO AN EDITOR)

THIS is not an answer to the lengthy review of *Criticism in America: Its Function and Status* in one of your recent issues. It is not an argument for the things in which I believe; nor is it, as it might well be, a protest and blast of defiance against all the writers who have done me the honour to discuss my work without doing me the honour to read what I have written. But a few of your readers will, I think, be interested to know what I do *not* believe, if for no other reason than that these things are exactly what some of my critics (including your reviewer) have supposed me to stand for:

1. I am *not* an advocate of "aestheticism," in criticism or anything else. I have tried to make it clear that I regard "aestheticism" as an even graver critical vice than "moralism."

2. I am *not* an advocate of "impressionism." I have tried to make it clear that I regard impressionism as no less inadequate than the dogmatism traditionally opposed to it.

Appendix

3. I do *not* believe that criticism is "expression" in the sense in which art is expression, or that the critic who merely expresses himself serves the true function of criticism. Mr. Mencken and others may or may not have deduced this from my books, but the very reverse is explicitly stated by me. In one of my essays I have elaborated the arguments of an imaginary impressionist who holds such views but only to confute him.

4. Naturally, therefore, I do *not* believe that criticism is an art in the sense in which poetry or painting is an art. On the few occasions on which I have referred to the "art of criticism," it is apparent, I think, that I am emphasising a side of criticism in which its kinship with art is most direct and real, that first stage of the critical process in which the critic attempts through his imagination to recapture the creative vision of the artist.

5. I do *not* believe that great writers are or need be without profound convictions. I know some people think that an artist is a man who has nothing to say and who writes in order to prove it; but not in this way have the great writers conceived of their art.

6. Finally, I do *not* deny that everything man does is subject to a moral judgment; I merely doubt the

relevance of such a judgment at a given "moment" of the spirit. Every act of man may also be subjected to an aesthetic judgment (is it or is it not beautiful?), but there are moments of the spirit when it is irrelevant and impertinent. When a modern French writer conceives of Napoleon as essentially a great lyric artist—that seems to me an irrelevance. And when one of the older writers of New England, John Quincy Adams, says he reads Shakespeare "only as a moral teacher" and conceives it to be the purpose of *Othello* to prove that it is a crime for a white woman to marry a Negro—that also seems to me an irrelevance!

Notes on the New Humanism [1]

(1913-1914)

I

IRVING BABBITT'S "MASTERS OF MODERN FRENCH CRITICISM"

THIS is a dignified and important book, and deserves a high welcome: all the more when we contrast its style, its interest in ideas, and its width of outlook with the literary studies that usually proceed from American universities. Here is a book without that preoccupation with scraps of texts and philological fragments, that crass dulness and imperviousness to ideas on the one hand, or that crude journalistic spirit, not even deserving the title of

[1] The first of these two Notes was published in the *Journal of Philosophy, Psychology, and Scientific Methods* in December, 1913, as a review of Professor Babbitt's *Masters of Modern French Criticism*. Professor Babbitt replied to this review in the same journal in April, 1914, in an article entitled "The Modern Spirit and Mr. Spingarn." My rejoinder, "The Ancient Spirit and Professor Babbitt," reprinted here, was published in the same journal in June, 1914. I have added running comment in the form of footnotes.

The New Humanism

dilettantism in any noble sense, on the other hand, which have for the most part characterised the work that has come from our institutions of higher learning. I am thinking, of course, more especially of the field of "modern languages" in its academic sense, in which it might almost be said that no work of creative scholarship has been accomplished since the days of Child and Ticknor. In an age when, as Sainte-Beuve said, "it seems that to edit an old book already published, or to print some insignificant scrap for the first time, is a more serious claim to esteem than to have a style and ideas," it is particularly fitting to give a cordial welcome to a book which displays an interest in style and which makes a valiant effort to grapple with ideas.

If we were to sum up the book in a phrase, we should say that in it Brunetière speaks English.[1] A

[1] Such resemblances are of little importance; but those who are interested in such matters will find that the seventeenth-century English critic, Thomas Rymer, affords a much closer parallel to Professor Babbitt's approach to literature than Brunetière, whose individual literary judgments, irrespective of his theories, are on quite a different plane. Like Professor Babbitt, for whom the highest form of perception is "inspired and imaginative common sense," Rymer judged literature "by the practice of the ancients and by the common sense of all ages," and asserted that essentially "common sense suffices." But the resemblance is far

nature so essentially French as Brunetière's could not use another tongue without altering its temperament in some measure; and Professor Babbitt, it is only fair to say, exhibits the divergence that such a sea-change imposes on him. But it is the tradition of French academic criticism that speaks throughout the book. The very critics selected are those that Brunetière himself would have selected as masters of his own art in his own country; the method of dealing with them is the method fixed, as it were, by him; the wailing cry for lost traditions, for old standards, for set *genres*, is unmistakably his. In both Brunetière and his American disciple we have the same confused dualism which attacks scientific naturalism in liter-

---

wider and more profound than this, and may be noted alike in their style and their miscellaneous learning, their ethical preoccupation, their insistence on standards and rules, their reverence for "decorum" or "poetical decency," and the ferocity of their dislike for everything that seems "romantic"; so that if Professor Babbitt had expressed some of his opinions in 1680,— to quote a sentence of his own about Mr. Dreiser,—"they would have been wrong, but they would at least have had the semblance of novelty." My own judgment of Rymer as a critic, which steers a middle course between the opposing opinions of Pope and Macaulay, will be found in the chapter devoted to him in the Introduction to my *Critical Essays of the Seventeenth Century*, to which students of the New Humanism may be referred.

ature and which in the very same breath defends
the wholly naturalistic theory of the literary *genre*.
Both are moralists, controversialists, pamphleteers,
rather than literary critics; both exhibit the same
suspicion of the imagination on its purely creative
side.

Take, for instance, Professor Babbitt's essay on
Scherer. The reader will search in vain for a single
allusion to literature or art, to the life of the imagination in any of its forms. He will find, instead, extended summaries of Scherer's views on relativity
and the absolute, on progress and humanity, on
Hegel and Napoleon. I have no fault to find with
these admirable paraphrases of an author's thought
on subjects that concern men at so many points, and
merely express a naïve wonder at a theory of literary
criticism that can be so inclusive as to find an interest
in every subject under the sun except imaginative
literature.

In the two chapters on Sainte-Beuve we might expect to find other preoccupations. Here indeed, we
say, criticism will find and express itself; contact with
this delicate and masterly spirit will encourage and
inspire an attitude more purely aesthetic. But what
do we actually find? It is the author's theory that

Appendix

the relationship of a great writer with his literary predecessors has little or no bearing on his own peculiar genius; yet here we find the most minute analysis of Sainte-Beuve's relations to his spiritual predecessors, to La Bruyère, La Rochefoucauld, Bayle, Horace, Montaigne, Vinet, and the rest. Professor Babbitt is constantly protesting against the tendency of criticism in "ceasing to be literary and becoming historical and biographical and scientific"; yet here we find the emphasis wholly laid on Sainte-Beuve's relation to his time, to romanticists and naturalists, to anything and everything, in a word, except his own peculiar art as a critic of literature. His actual criticism of any poet, novelist, or other writer is passed over lightly with the quotation of an *obiter dictum* or an epigram; there is no attempt to analyse a single essay of the greatest critic with whom this book has to deal.

We assume that this is what our author means when he tells us in his preface that he has not tried "to criticise criticism, at best a somewhat languid business, but to criticise critics, which may be a far more legitimate task." But what is it fair to ask of an essay on any great literary critic? His theories of Hegel and Napoleon, of progress and humanity, or his successes and failure in understanding and interpreting the great writers and in enriching our comprehension of the true nature of art? May we not ask to have questions like these answered for us: How has he done his work; how has he made us understand the greatness of a great book or see the littleness of a little one; what do art and criticism mean for him? But we might read these two chapters on Sainte-Beuve from start to finish without knowing the art of a single one of his own essays, his conception of the nature of poetry or criticism, his method of approaching a single author concretely, his genius in unraveling the difficult tangles of another man's genius. For this task of criticising critics there is needed the same kind of insight, critical insight, as in the original operation of the critic in criticising poets and novelists; and the fact is that Professor Babbitt is entirely lacking in this insight. He is a defender of tradition, an historian of ideas and tendencies, a moralist of considerable power, a populariser of general ideas; anything and everything, in fact, except a critic or a student of criticism.

His book suffers also in another way, from the lack of a unified attitude toward his central theme. The fact is that Professor Babbitt has no aesthetic theory, or at least has expounded none in this book. He has shown that the critic's right to judge is part of the whole philosophical problem of our time, and he has much advice to give on questions of critical practise: that criticism today needs "standards," that judgment and selection must be added to taste, that tradition and the classics need more attention, that scientific positivism must be destroyed, that critical appreciation must be curbed this side of "superlativism." These he espouses with a masculine eloquence worthy of the best traditions of academic criticism. But to the questions—What is art? What is literature? What is criticism?—he offers no answers; and he has no answer for the simple reason that he has never asked himself any of these questions in precisely this form. His utterances are controlled, not by any unified and consistent thought in the field of aesthetics or critical theory, but by a moral theory which is the expression of his personal bias in respect to the practical needs of the culture of today. In fine, if we might give the book the extended title which was common in works of its kind in the seventeenth century, it would read somewhat after this fashion: "A Discourse on the Intellectual and Literary Troubles of our Times: In the form of a running comment on certain modern French critics; Together with a discussion of the various confusions of thought current in our day; To which the Author has added some of his own."

II

THE ANCIENT SPIRIT AND PROFESSOR BABBITT

Some time ago I had the pleasure of reviewing Professor Babbitt's *Masters of Modern French Criticism* in this journal; and in a recent issue he has published a courteous reply under the title of "The Modern Spirit and Mr. Spingarn."

Professor Babbitt is much disturbed by my statement that his book lacks "unified and consistent thought" and represents largely "personal bias." I am not certain whether his reply is intended to confirm or refute this statement, since the ideas which he now expresses are exactly those on which I based my original contention. He restates briefly what he had already said in the preface of his book, and I must therefore assume that we are to accept all this as proof of "consistent thought." But consistent thought about what? If he will turn again to my review, he will find this assertion: "The fact is that

Appendix

Professor Babbitt has no aesthetic theory. . . . To the questions—What is art? What is literature? What is criticism?—he offers no answers." In his recent reply he does not touch these questions at any point. He explains that literary criticism has much the same problems to face as modern philosophy, that it, too, must deal with the antitheses of intellectualism and intuitionalism, of discipline and anarchy, and so on; and he implies that ideas of this kind vindicate the consistency of his thought in the field of aesthetic theory and criticism.

I confess, however, that if these utterances are intended as answers to the questions—What is art? What is criticism?—they are not unlike the answer that my five-year-old son recently gave to the question—What is arithmetic? "It is when you say one and one make two, two and two make four, three and three make six." My son has obviously identified arithmetic and stated some of its problems; he has explained it exactly as we explain anything which we have to face and concerning which we have no "unified and consistent thought." Professor Babbitt, however, has hardly gone so far as to identify criticism in any way that indicates its essential purposes or processes; he has simply stated some of the prob-

lems that confront it at this period of time.[1] He is
under an illusion when he thinks that his "principles"
seem negligible to me merely because they are "too
different" from my own to make comprehension possible. I do not disagree with his principles, if by this
is meant principles peculiar to aesthetics and criticism
as distinguished from principles of ethics or philosophy in general; I merely find none with which to
agree or disagree. I agree with his statement of some
of the *problems* of modern criticism, just as I disagree with statement of others; but I have looked in
vain for any indication that he has asked himself
what art really is, what literature really is, or what
criticism really is. It seems to me fair to say of such

[1] It is only fair to say that Professor Babbitt had asserted a
fundamental, and to my mind valid, principle when he defended
the possibility and the value of judgment against impressionists
in criticism and intuitionalists in philosophy; but he left un-
touched the specific question that after all is the chief concern of
criticism: Judgment of and about what? This again confirms
what I tried to bring out in the sentences that follow, with
perhaps a justifiable touch of exaggeration, that Professor Babbitt in this book had an ethical theory, perhaps a general philosophy of a sort, but no aesthetic theory. I should now prefer
to say, on the basis of his other books, that his aesthetic theory
is vitiated by moralistic and intellectualistic errors, but that his
cultural value, as I have pointed out above, is considerable.

Appendix

a book that it lacks unified and consistent thought in
the field of literary criticism.

Professor Babbitt does, however, criticise the aesthetic theory of others, and I think that here, too, he
has shown his confusion of ethical bias with aesthetic
thought. He assumes, for example, that the theory of
Benedetto Croce, that expression is art, implies of
necessity a lack of that intellectual discipline which he
regards as the chief need of the culture of our time.[1]

[1] I realize the inadequacy of the explanation of Croce's theory
that follows. A more adequate explanation, Croce's own, would
be that the contrast which Professor Babbitt develops in his
other books between *expression* ("something vital and expansive")
and *form* ("felt rather as a limiting and circumscribing law")
is merely an imperfect statement of Croce's own contrast between *impression* ("sentiment" or "material") and *expression*
("form" or "lyrical intuition"). For Croce art is the unity of
these two moments, by which form resolves the material into
itself; and Professor Babbitt also admits that "the problem of
mediating between these two terms . . . must be solved in some
way if beauty is to be achieved in any way relevant to man."
His own dualism is thus transcended in art, as humanity seeks
to transcend all dualisms, for of course there are no pure dualists
or pure monists any more than there are pure optimists or pure
pessimists. Croce's term, "expression" (for which he uses the
equivalents, "form" and "lyrical intuition," or as it might just
as well be called, with special reference to the need of our day,
"epic intuition") does not represent the "expansive" element
in art; for this element Croce uses the term "impression," or its
equivalents, "sentiment" and "material," as is most clearly in-

The New Humanism

If we assume that all expression is art, he argues,
there is no place for training, for discipline, for tradition, for ideals, for culture; there is nothing left but
anarchy. Nothing could be farther from the truth.
Disciplined art and undisciplined art are both art;
or perhaps we˘should rather say that disciplined
minds as well as undisciplined ones may express

dicated in his *Nuovi Saggi di Estetica.* But these are problems
that are ignored, or touched upon only in a negative way, in
the *Masters of Modern French Criticism*, with which these Notes
are exclusively concerned, or my discussion of it would have
assumed a quite different form. If it were still necessary to
discuss the New Humanism, and if I were writing today with
Professor Babbitt's other books in mind, I should take issue with
various aspects of his attitude toward the arts, with his crude
dualism, with his naïve idea that Aristotle's doctrine of the
"mean" sums up all ethical speculation and that Aristotle's "The
end is the chief thing of all" is the last word of philosophy,
and with other things too numerous to mention in a footnote.
I should also point out the absurdity of writing a history of
Rousseau's influence, as Professor Babbitt has done in *Rousseau
and Romanticism*, without a single mention of Hegel's *Phenom-
enology of the Spirit*, which contains the most powerful attack
on Rousseauism ever written, a century before Lasserre gave
the cue to Professor Babbitt. Nor is the mention of Hegel in-
apposite in connection with the new cult of Confucius and
Buddha, for when a similar exaggerated Orientalism showed
itself at the beginning of the nineteenth century, Hegel's comment in substance was this: "Why look so far? All that Confucius says has been said, and better said, in the *De Officiis* of
Cicero."

themselves in art. The mistake into which he has fallen is obvious: he is framing his definition, not from the thing itself, but from what he believes to be the best form of it. But bad English is English as much as good English; the art of a child is art quite as much as that of Michelangelo.[1] It may be important to distinguish between the two and to encourage the former at the expense of the latter; but the writer

[1] Professor Babbitt has misrepresented this sentence on several occasions by citing only half of it and wresting it from its context. This half-sentence, "The art of a child is art quite as much as thàt of Michelangelo," by itself, and understood as Professor Babbitt would have it understood, may perhaps be justly characterised even by the barbaric term "primitivistic." But the rest of the sentence, and the sentence which precedes it, give it quite a different meaning: "The mistake into which he has fallen is obvious: he is framing his definition, not from the thing itself, but from what he believes to be the best form of it. But bad English is English as much as good English; the art of a child is art quite as much as that of Michelangelo." This conception of a definition may be true or false, but the last half-sentence certainly loses its real meaning when torn from its context, and especially when "the art of a child" is no longer correlated with "bad English." Further light on its real meaning, and on my attitude towards "primitivism," may be obtained from my remarks on anthropology in "The New Criticism." Professor Babbitt himself insists that "if we are to do justice to Plato's theory of inspiration we must interpret it in the total spirit of his writings," and it is to be regretted that he has so consistently failed to follow his own excellent admonition except in the case of Plato.

on aesthetics should at least understand what they have in common in that both are expression and therefore art. A disciplined mind will express itself differently from an undisciplined one; but until the artist expresses himself he cannot create art, and when he expresses himself he has created it. Professor Babbitt imagines that this conception of art must necessarily indicate a preference for the undisciplined form; but it is after all merely an attempt to understand what art really is, and nothing else. It is not an attempt to give practical advice to the men and women of our own time.

Professor Babbitt complains, with more apparent justification, that I have done him an injustice in saying that in his essay on Scherer there is not a "single allusion to literature or art, to the life of the imagination in any of its forms." He insists that in his essay he has discussed Scherer's attitude toward Molière, Sainte-Beuve, Zola, Baudelaire, Goethe, and others. I turn to the passage on Molière, and I find that the author of *Tartuffe* is mentioned in order to justify a quotation from Scherer in regard to—the deficiencies of the French language in the later nineteenth century. I turn to the passage on Zola, and I find that an excerpt from Scherer's essay on Zola is quoted in regard to—the vulgarising influence of democracy on culture. Is it unfair to say that these are not allusions to "literature or art, to the life of the imagination in any of its forms"? Is it unfair to say that Professor Babbitt is not concerned, in any of these passages, with the way in which criticism interprets creation, but that he is wholly obsessed with the problems of modern culture on their practical side?

This is what Professor Babbitt is interested in, and this alone. He does not care what art or criticism is, but he does care that young men and women should have discipline, training, tradition, ideals. Despite his assertion that he is "reacting in the name of the modern spirit," his mind is still in the period of Graeco-Roman culture, when literature was simply regarded as a preparation for the more important activities of life; and as Quintilian in writing a book on the Orator really wrote a treatise on the education of Roman youth, so Professor Babbitt in writing about modern French critics has really written a treatise on our system of academic or literary education. His book is a contribution to American culture; it is, as I have said, a dignified and valuable book; but it adds little to our knowledge of the history or theory of criticism. If Professor Babbitt is inclined to take this statement too seriously, I can only remind him that Burton's *Anatomy of Melancholy*, while adding little to our knowledge of psychology, and *Gulliver's Travels*, while adding nothing to our knowledge of geography, lose little if any of their interest on this account.

A Note on French Scholarship[1]

Every young scholar dreams of a magnum opus
which is destined never to be written; and in
the days of my own apprenticeship I had the temerity
to dream of two. One was to be a great history of

[1] This scholarly fragment would have been left to slumber
in the *Romanic Review* of January, 1926, where it originally
appeared, if it were not for the extensive controversy which
it excited in France on the general question of the methods of
literary history. It is a review of a French work of scholarship
(M. Magendie's *La politesse mondaine et les théories de l'honnêteté en France au XVIIᵉ siècle*), and my strictures on it disturbed the equanimity even of the Sorbonne. The controversy
that followed has furnished the subject of a special monograph
by M. Philippe Van Tieghem (*Tendances nouvelles en histoire
littéraire*, Paris, 1930). But much of the controversy seems to
me wide of the mark, for my review does not touch the question of literary history or criticism as such. It is concerned solely
with a phase of the history of culture, and with obvious defects
of scholarship in dealing with that phase; the history of imaginative literature presents a quite different problem from the history of social ideals. My chief justification for reprinting this
paper, which has so little in common with the rest of this volume, is the hope that it may stimulate some one to write the
history of the ideal of the gentleman which was so long in my
thoughts; and if he is worthy of so fine a subject, he will not
permit himself to be immersed in the minutiae and side issues
on which a review of a learned book naturally insists.

criticism and literary theory from the Greeks to our own day, a dream which even the appearance of the first volume of Saintsbury's *History of Criticism* did not completely destroy; and the other, to which I sometimes gave the fanciful title of "The Birth and Death of the Gentleman," was to be a history of social ideals, as summed up in the word "gentleman," from the days of chivalry to the days of American democracy. To the first of these I have made some fitful contributions during the years that have since elapsed; but the other project is recorded only in a few fragmentary and negligible studies, beginning with a review of Opdycke's translation of Castiglione's *Cortegiano* in the *Nation* in 1902 and ending with the editing of an Elizabethan version of Della Casa's *Galateo* in 1913. Of all the fifteen years of study which I devoted to this subject, nothing remains except the two hundred volumes, more or less, which still gather dust in my library,—volumes which bear such various titles as *Il Gentilhuomo, Della Ingiustitia del Duello, Della Natura d'Amore, Dialogo de' Giuochi senesi, Diálogo de la Verdadera Honra Militar, La Maison des Jeux, L'Honneste Femme, Traité de la Cour, The Boke of Curtasye, The Compleat Gentleman,* and *The Broad Stone of Honour.*

Appendix

It was therefore with considerable interest, and no little humility, that I approached M. Magendie's ponderous tome, which housed a fragment of my youthful dream. It is no mere figure of speech to call a volume of 943 pages ponderous. Its subject is the "honnête homme," the French gentleman of the seventeenth century, more especially the theory of social conduct as expressed in the theoretical treatises of the period; and to describe and explain this minor aspect of the life of sixty years M. Magendie has employed about half a million words, which is approximately the number M. Lanson uses to sum up the whole history of French literature, and almost twice as many as Windelband uses to sum up the whole of European philosophy. I am instituting no invidious comparisons. M. Magendie's aim is wholly different from theirs, and the question is whether he has really justified the use of his enormous framework.

In the days when the two dreams were still real for me, I entertained a very high regard for French doctoral dissertations, of which this volume appears to be a modern example. I used to contrast their maturity and intelligence with the immaturity and unintelligence of doctoral dissertations emanating

from other countries that I might mention. I have
not kept track of them for many years, but this work
and others like it make me wonder whether I did
not overestimate their value. Perhaps I was thinking of a few high spots, like Renan's monograph on
Averroës and Averroism, and judging the practice
from the exceptional work of genius; or perhaps the
general standard has fallen; I am not in a position
to decide. Not a few of those which I have seen im-
press me as exhibiting anything but maturity and intelligence. Too often, as in this case, they are swollen
and distended, like a balloon; and one searches in
vain for that illumination of reason and that con-
cision of style which we connect with the very nature
of the French spirit.[1]

[1] Many years before this I had publicly expressed my youthful enthusiasm for the culture of France, "where scholarship
is so broad, so lucid, and so sane." I had attended the International Congress of History at Paris in the summer of 1900,
with the intention of reading a scholarly paper before the section on literary history. But after listening to a succession of
learned monographs I grew impatient of this massing of erudition; and when my turn came, I cast aside the paper I had
prepared and spoke more or less extemporaneously on the purpose and methods of literary scholarship with special reference to the immediate needs of the United States. A few days
later the chairman of the section, M. Gustave Lanson, asked me
for a copy of my speech, and I hastily wrote a brief summary,

Appendix

M. Magendie has poured out all his note-books on the printed page; he has omitted nothing that he has learnt. I do not wish to make light of his patient research nor to wage indiscriminate war on erudition in general, such as is fashionable today among journalists but is out of place on the lips of a scholar. I mean merely to imply that a scholar may do more with his material than to give long abstracts of all the books he has read, and to arrange these abstracts in chronological order, with occasional interludes of comment on their historical meaning. It would be

which was published in the Proceedings of the Congress in 1901. In this address I attacked the excessive specialization of American scholarship, which imitated the vices rather than the virtues of German culture ("Our scholars have become mere machines, tabulating facts, counting syllables"), pleaded for a broader conception of scholarship, and concluded: "Our country was discovered by both Germanic and Latin races, and we demand a share of the culture of both. We cannot be satisfied with German culture by itself, and I hope you will pardon me when I say that French culture by itself cannot suffice us either. The originality of American scholarship may well consist in the perfect union of the two." Benedetto Croce wrote me at the time: "You have indicated admirably what American scholars should attempt to accomplish; but would it not be well for all of us Europeans to be a little *American* in the sense in which you speak?"; and he again expressed his sympathy with the ideas of this youthful address in the first volume of his journal, *La Critica*, in 1903 (see his *Problemi di Estetica*, 1910, page 78).

unfair to say that M. Magendie has done no more than this; he has distinguished between various aspects of his subject, and made us realise, among other things, how the conception of life of the bourgeoisie and the moralists who expressed its ideals differed from that of the aristocrats and the imaginative writers who sought to please them. His main achievement, however, consists in the fact that he has read a great many important and unimportant books, most of them difficult to procure, and has made their contents accessible to all who may care to know about them. I, for one, am grateful to him for all this information.

But unfortunately, despite his patient research and his 943 pages, he has not read enough. In his bibliography, which covers thirty pages, I merely note in passing, as a minor matter, that among the modern works dealing with the subject he includes only one not written in French. In the body of his book he mentions half a dozen early foreign books on social life, such as Castiglione's *Cortegiano*, Della Casa's *Galateo*, Guazzo's *Civil Conversazione*, and Erasmus's *De Civilitate morum puerilium*, all available in French translation; he briefly describes their contents, and then airily dismisses them. He devotes a

Appendix

page to refuting Toldo's contention that the Chevalier de Méré was directly indebted to the *Cortegiano*. But to prove or disprove individual borrowing is wholly beside the point. For the fact is that the theories of "honnêteté" current in France in the first half of the seventeenth century had been fully developed by the Italian social theorists of the sixteenth century, quite as completely as the classical rules of French criticism had been anticipated by Scaliger and Castelvetro, Minturno and Piccolomini. The social customs of the Précieuses and their successors had been determined in virtually all their detail by the courts and academies of Mantua, Ferrara, Siena, Urbino, and Milan; indeed, the Marquise de Rambouillet, who played so important a part in transferring these social customs as a body to the soil of France, was herself born in Rome and was half-Italian. No study of the history of the ideal of the gentleman is possible without an understanding of its progressive modification, from the "knight" of French chivalry, through the Italian "courtier," with his classical culture, the later Renaissance "gentiluomo," and the French "honnête homme," not to mention the minor transitional stages of French "galant" and Spanish "caballero," until the English conception of the "gentleman" conquered the world. Nor can any of these phases of the history of the gentleman be rightly apprehended without a study of the growth of the conception of "honour," that new ethical ideal which gives savour to them all and is the immortal heritage of mediaeval chivalry and romance. To ignore these facts, and the literature that has grown out of these facts, is to misconceive completely the history of social ideals in France and in the whole of Europe.

If M. Magendie had been familiar with the work of a single American scholar, Professor T. F. Crane, more especially the recent book on *Italian Social Customs of the Sixteenth Century, and Their Influence on the Literature of Europe*, he could never have been satisfied with so narrow a perspective. Professor Crane's book deals with only a single aspect of this great problem, the social amusements and "parlour games" of the Italians of the Cinquecento. It omits all the more general discussions of social theory, such as Muzio's *Il Gentilhuomo* and Possevino's *Dialogo dell'Onore*; it is, like M. Magendie's work, a collection of abstracts of books arranged chronologically rather than a searching historical study. But it indicates the nature of France's debt to Italy in some-

thing of its true light, and this M. Magendie has
wholly failed to do. For example, Sorel's *Maison des
Jeux* and Mademoiselle de Scudéry's *Les Jeux* (pre-
fixed to her romance, *Mathilde d'Aguilar*) owe their
origin to books like Ringhieri's *Cento Giuochi liberali
e d'Ingegno* and Bargagli's *Trattenimenti*, which are
typical expressions of the social life of Italy in the
latter part of the sixteenth century. Ringhieri's book
had been partially translated into French; he is actually mentioned (as "messer Innocent Rhingier") in
one of the works which M. Magendie has read, the
Maison des Jeux; yet even this did not whet M.
Magendie's curiosity, and the reader of his book will
look in vain for any discussion of Ringhieri or Bargagli.

But to add illustrations of this sort would add
nothing to the argument; the fault with M. Magendie's book is not a question of details. He has
studied a great social problem and a body of social
theories without any real understanding of their
provenance or their place in history. Because of his
ignorance of these antecedents, he has been unable
to explain the exact nature of France's contribution
to civilisation—what was original in her work as well
as what was merely borrowed. If the swollen pages

of his book would seem to indicate that French scholarship has lost something of its organising power and its gift of succinct and illuminating narrative, this lack of European perspective would seem to indicate a form of inbreeding from which French scholarship must escape if it would understand the meaning of history and make that meaning clear to the world of letters. It would be indeed a tragedy if scholars could no longer look to France for those striking and original gifts of interpretation which she, and she alone, has been able to give us.

The Seven Arts and the Seven Confusions [1]

THERE are as many arts as there are artists,—the number is not seven, but countless as the stars. We group them in constellations for our convenience, not theirs; seven units are more easily handled than a trillion. The confusions in regard to them are countless too; the actual number is far greater; but they may also be gathered for our convenience into seven groups,—"seven" has the perfume of a mystic tradition kept fragrant by the superstition of generations of men. So I begin with a roll-call of them all: Poets

[1] This essay, first printed in the *Seven Arts* in March, 1917, merely represents another and lighter form of "The New Criticism," and most of it was incorporated in that and other essays of *Creative Criticism* later in the same year, while this dismembered relic was left to die in the periodical in which it had first appeared. If I reprint it now in an Appendix, it is because, while I was overseas during the War and could not be consulted, it was given renewed currency in Mr. Ludwig Lewisohn's collection, *A Modern Book of Criticism*, in the "Modern Library," but disfigured by misprints that completely distort my meaning, and it has seemed to me that it should at least be available in its correct form.

write for money; poets are influenced by their environment; poets write in metres; poets write tragedies and comedies; poets are moral or immoral; poets are democratic or aristocratic; poets use figures of speech.

The first of the Seven Confusions, then, is this, that "poets write for money." This is only one way of stating a misconception of the nature of art that might be phrased in a hundred different ways. The most common form today is perhaps this: "Plays are written to be acted, not read." The confusion remains exactly the same when it is put: "Plays are written to be read, not acted." We are not concerned with the fact (if it be a fact) but with its implication for criticism.

The poet may find that a brisk walk stimulates his writing, or that he can write more easily when he has smoked a cigarette. The walk or the cigarette has not produced the poetry; it has simply served as a stimulus to the personality that creates the poetry. It opens the faucet, but neither produces nor modifies the water that pours out. Other poets find that they cannot write easily without the stimulus of imagined reward—money, the plaudits of the crowd, the resplendent beauty of theatrical performance.

Appendix

But men with the same ambitions write different poems or plays, and in this difference lies the real secret of art. For after all, whatever the imaginary stimulus, there is only one real urge in the poet's soul, to express what is in him, and so make manifest his vision of life. To trifle with the plumbing, after the faucet has been turned on, instead of drinking the water, is hardly the function of the critic or the lover of art. To say, therefore, that poets write for money, that playwrights write for the stage, that painters paint to be "hung," is to confuse mere stimulus with creative impulse.

The second confusion, that "poets are the products of their environment," is a twisted corollary of the first. We need not quarrel with the statement so long as it remains suspended in the air, as a vague generalisation that can do no harm unless it carries with it the further implication that a study of the environment helps us to understand the poetry. Not what the poet's environment may have been, but what he has made out of it, is what interests us in a poem. The secret of a unique personality (if one may use the phrase when personality means nothing but uniqueness) is what the reader enjoys and the critic seeks to discover. Sociologists may trouble themselves about external and superficial resemblances between artists or groups of artists; aesthetic critics are concerned only with the unbridgeable differences. To look for a poet's power outside of his work rather than in it, to assume that his relation to his environment is of any concern whatever to a lover or critic of poetry, is to confuse criticism and sociology.

The most deeply imbedded superstition in regard to art, however, is concerned with its external form. The third confusion, that "poets write in metres," is therefore one of the oldest of all the confusions. Aesthetic theorists have waged a battle against it, from the days of Aristotle, who said that poetry is distinguished from history by something more essential than metre, and that the history of Herodotus would remain history even if written in verse, to our own day, when Benedetto Croce, the only modern who may be mentioned in the same breath with him, has left the old confusion without any ground to stand on. The fact is that there is no real distinction between prose and verse. Out of the infinite varieties of rhythm in human speech, it is possible, for convenience' sake, to separate the more regular from the more irregular, and to call one verse and the other prose: to say where one ends and the other begins is impossible. But to build a system on these empirical and convenient classifications is to confuse superficial likenesses with the realities of creative art. For after all no two poets write in the same metre. I may imagine that I am writing an iambic pentameter, or a line with a certain succession of beats or accents, but in reality I am creating a new line. If that line is good it is because of some special virtue of its own, and not because of some imaginary and purely external resemblance to something else. Poets do not use old metres, but each poet creates rhythms of his own.

What is true of metre is also true of language itself. To speak of "learning a language" is to risk the danger of the same confusion; we do not learn language, we learn how to create it. That is why it is so wide of the mark to say, as Max Eastman does, that to "sail into a man" is or is not a good expression because it means the same as the Latinism "to inveigh against a man." "Inveigh" may etymologically mean "sail into"; but if language is a living thing— a form of art, not to be torn from its context or understood outside of it—the Latin word helps to explain the English as much as the disinterred skeleton of a thirteenth century English yeoman helps us to understand the personality of Max Eastman. It is inconceivable that a modern thinker should still adhere to abstract tests of good expression, when it is obvious that we can only tell whether it is good or bad when we see it in its natural context. Is any word artistically bad in itself? Is not "ain't" an excellent expression when placed in the mouth of an illiterate character in a play or story? To deal with abstract classification instead of the real thing—versification instead of poetry, grammar instead of language, technique instead of painting—is to be guilty of confusing form as concrete expression with form as a dead husk.

The fourth confusion may be summed up in the phrase: "Poets write tragedies or comedies." It is true that poets set out with the intention of writing them, although they have only the vaguest idea of what they mean by the terms; and it is equally true that their work may be impeded by false conceptions of these literary forms. But fortunately for us, their real achievement is independent of this confused ambition. Tragedy, comedy, lyric, epic, and other words of this sort, are simply convenient ways of classifying works of art, just as books may be classified as tall or small, cloth-bound or morocco-bound, for the purpose of arrangement in libraries, or men may be classified as tall or small for the purpose of arrangement in a company of soldiers. We shall always find these terms useful, in poetry no less than in libraries or regiments, and the confusion arises only when it is implied (as is almost always implied) that the classification is not merely a matter of convenience, but a law of art by which poems are to be judged. For example, a critic studies a number of poems having a certain resemblance and called tragedies; out of this study he evolves a "law of tragedy" and then attempts to impose it on the first poet who writes another poem of somewhat the same kind. "Sir," we hear him say throughout the ages, "you have disregarded all the laws of good tragedy, and your poem is therefore no good." The poet's answer should be a very simple one: "There are no laws of good tragedy; there are only good or bad poems." No rule, no theory, no "law" coined by critics or scholars has any validity for the poet in the creative act; and when that act is completed and the poem achieved, the critic must make his theory of tragedy chime with the new poet's poem, not the poem with the theory. Only in one sense has any of these terms any profound significance, and that is the use of the word "lyric" to represent the free expressiveness of all art. The *Divine Comedy, Lear,* Michelangelo's David, a Corot landscape, or a Bach fugue is as truly lyric as any of the songs of Heine or Shelley.

The fifth confusion, that "poets are moral or immoral," is also world-old. We should no longer banish poets from an ideal Republic because of the immorality of their art, as Plato did, but most of us still confuse art with morals. To say that poetry is moral or immoral is as meaningless as to say that an equilateral triangle is moral and an isosceles triangle immoral. Surely we must realise the absurdity of testing anything by a standard which does not belong to it or a purpose for which it was not intended. Imagine these whiffs of conversation at a dinner table: "This cauliflower would be excellent if it had only been prepared in accordance with international law." "Do you know why the cook's pastry is so good? He has never told a lie or seduced a woman." But why multiply obvious examples? We do not concern ourselves with morals when we test the engineer's bridge or the scientist's researches; indeed we go farther, and say that it is the moral duty of the scientist to disregard morals in his search for truth. As a man he may be judged by moral standards, but the truth of his conclusions can only be judged by the standard of science. Beauty's world is remote from both these standards; she aims neither at morals nor at truth. Her imaginary creations, by definition, make no pretense to reality, and cannot be judged by reality's tests. Art is expression, and poets succeed or fail by their success or failure in completely and perfectly expressing themselves. If the ideals they express are not the ideals we admire most, we must blame not the poets but ourselves; in the world where morals count we have failed to give them the proper material out of which to rear a nobler edifice. To separate art and morality is not to destroy moral values but to augment them—to give them increased powers and a new freedom in the realm in which they have the right to reign.

In modern America it would be strange if our practical hopes did not lead us into a sixth confusion, that "poets are democratic or aristocratic,"—as if art were concerned with the political programme of the poet any more than with his moral standards. It is easy to sneer at Shakespeare and Dante as "reactionaries," but it is difficult to see what this has to do with the quality of their poetry, unless we are to assume that only men of our own political or economic convictions can be good poets. It is as hard to write a good poem on democracy as on aristocracy; also, it would seem even harder, if we may judge from the experience of poets. To find fault with the past because it is not exactly like the present is as good a test as one needs of a shallow mind; and to find fault with good poetry because it is not .good political science or good sociology is a fairly serviceable test of the incompetent critic. It is not the purpose of poetry to further the cause of democracy, or any other practical "cause," any more than it is the purpose of bridge-building to further the cause of Esperanto. If a poet consecrates himself to the spread of democratic ideals, his work still remains to be tested by the standards of art, not of politics. Criticism is concerned with the question, "Has he written a good poem?" and is not helped in its decision by the answer to a wholly different and indifferent question: "Is he a democrat, a conservative, a socialist, or a psychoanalyst?"

Somewhat similar is the attempt of critics to determine the subject-matter of poetry, no less than the political convictions of poets. It is an old illusion: in the seventeenth century, for example, Boileau belaboured the poets who had the temerity to prefer

Appendix

Christian to Greek mythology. Today the critics are insisting on the use of contemporary material, and are praising the poets whose subjects are drawn from the life of their own time. But even if it were possible for critics to impose subjects on poets, how can the poets deal with anything but contemporary material? How can a twentieth century poet, even when he imagines that he is concerned with early Greek or Egyptian life, deal with any subject but the life of his own time, except in the most external and superficial detail? Cynical critics have said since the first outpouring of men's hearts, "There is nothing new in art; there are no new subjects for the poets." But the very reverse is true. There are no old subjects; every subject is new as soon as it has been transformed by the imagination of the poet.

Finally, there is the confusion which is represented by the statement that "poets write metaphors." Poets write a good many things, so many that it is hard to say what they do write; frequently they even write nonsense; but one thing we may be sure they do not write, and that is the impossible. Metaphors are myths created by grammarians which have no reality in the poet's world or any other. The misconception involved in these "figures of speech" is that style is something separate from the work of art and not part and parcel of its inner being. It is conceived as an ornament to be added to or subtracted from expression instead of as expression itself. If "lionhearted" be only another way of saying "brave," why use one rather than the other? Or if they mean something different, however slight, why say that one is used for the other at all? We have inherited these figures from the old Greek rhetoricians, and in any theory of style as concrete expression they have no place. Every phrase is a thing in itself, always indefinably new, wherever it may be, never representing anything but itself in the exact context where it is found for the first and only time. It can never be exactly the same, even when it is used again in the same passage; and it has been well said that the word "love" in Dante's famous line,

"Amor, che a nullo amato amar perdona,"

is not the same word thrice repeated, but must be considered artistically as three separate and distinct expressions.

The misconception involved in all these "confusions" is the same—it is to mistake anatomy for personality, the husk for the core, the dead for the living, abstractions for realities, non-art for art.